fermentation
revolution

fermentation revolution

70 easy, healthy recipes for sauerkraut, kombucha, kimchi and more

SÉBASTIEN BUREAU AND DAVID CÔTÉ

For complete cataloguing information, see page 207.

Disclaimer

The recipes in this book have been carefully tested by our kitchen and our tasters. To the best of our knowledge, they are safe and nutritious for ordinary use and users. For those people with food or other allergies, or who have special food requirements or health issues, please read the suggested contents of each recipe carefully and determine whether or not they may create a problem for you. All recipes are used at the risk of the consumer.

We cannot be responsible for any hazards, loss or damage that may occur as a result of any recipe use.

For those with special needs, allergies, requirements or health problems, in the event of any doubt, please contact your medical adviser prior to the use of any recipe.

Translator: Donna Vekteris
Editor: Sue Sumeraj
Recipe editor: Jennifer MacKenzie
Proofreader: Kelly Jones
Indexer: Gillian Watts
Production: Alicia McCarthy/PageWave Graphics Inc.
Photography: Mathieu Dupuis
Food stylist: Luce Meunier

Page layout adapted from *Révolution Fermentation,* designed by Ann-Sophie Caouette.

Cover image: Lactofermented Root Vegetables (page 42)

The publisher gratefully acknowledges the financial support of our publishing program by the Government of Canada through the Canada Book Fund.

Canadä

Published by Robert Rose Inc.
120 Eglinton Avenue East, Suite 800, Toronto, Ontario, Canada M4P 1E2
Tel: (416) 322-6552 Fax: (416) 322-6936
www.robertrose.ca

Printed and bound in Canada

1 2 3 4 5 6 7 8 9 TCP 26 25 24 23 22 21 20 19 18

Contents

FOREWORD: The Hymn to Life, the song of the revolution

THE WORLD IS LIFE. The air, the earth, wood, water, your hands, the kitchen counter, the door handle, plants — even plastic ones — are coated in life. Bacteria, yeast and microorganisms of all kinds live, thrive and proliferate. They digest, transform, catalyze, construct and simplify. These imperceptible creatures that are constantly creating are the players in a perpetual revolution. Without their presence, trees cannot grow, human beings cannot digest, life cannot develop and...grapes cannot turn into wine!

Bacteria are misunderstood, often feared and generally perceived as an enemy that must be vanquished at all costs. In fact, the real enemy is a lack of understanding of the invisible and a need to "oversterilize," ostensibly to safeguard health. This book is not a cookbook, but a hymn to microscopic life. It is an ode to mold, bacteria, fungi and all the living things surrounding us that want nothing more than to benefit us. To make them our allies and use their resources is somewhat revolutionary.

This book was not written for a clique of laboratory nerds, a handful of militant raw vegans or know-it-all gourmets (although it does address these three groups, because we do strive to avoid discriminating!). It's for those of us who don't wince at the idea of accommodating new micro-roommates under our roof, who happily imagine a food transformed before our eyes through the simple laws of nature, who still don't know what to do with the leftover vegetables in our fridge, who know somewhere deep inside that eating what lives is the source of life itself.

If you are holding this book in your hands, it means you are ready for a peaceful revolution inspired by the wisdom of the past to better prepare you for the future. All that's left for you to do is dive into this new, unsettling but fascinating world and discover the delicious experimental poem whose uncontested muse is fermentation!

Seb and David

INTRODUCTION: History, SCIENCE and Other Stuff You're Not Really Required to Read

ANY SELF-RESPECTING BOOK SHOULD HAVE a nice chapter that demonstrates the authors know what they're talking about. These pages gather together the modest academic knowledge we've acquired over time — not just through reading, but mainly through experimentation, trial and error, and our sweetest successes in the science of fermentation. We think you'll find these pages quite enjoyable to read, especially if you wish to understand how the fermentation process works. We won't, however, try to convince you that you need intimate knowledge of the origin and strain of certain bacteria in order to succeed with your cheese or sauerkraut. If you are champing at the bit to chop up your vegetables and see them be magically transformed, you have our permission to skip these pages of fermented prose and jump ahead to the actual recipes. If you find yourself in a conundrum along the way, you can always come back and browse through this chapter to find the answers to your questions.

TO FEAST, THEY HAD TO FERMENT

The most popular fermentations of yesterday and today did not appear by design by master chefs — they came about through error and lucky coincidences. Cheese, beer, wine, sauerkraut and kefir are basically fortuitous accidents that turned out so well, people wanted more. It is very likely that the first beer bubbles appeared in a bowl of barley forgotten in the rain somewhere in Egypt; that the pungent flavor of sauerkraut was first enjoyed by one of the thousands of laborers who built the Great Wall of China and had nothing but cabbage to eat; that kefir grains formed in a gourd made by a nomad from the skin of a yak in the Gobi Desert; that somewhere in Asia, a woman noticed that her cup of sweetened tea, forgotten a few days earlier on a windowsill, contained a tangy effervescent liquid now known as kombucha. As fermentation worked its magic in different civilizations, it had a powerful influence on these civilizations' cultures and destinies, opening up a world of possibilities for preserving food, making it more digestible and increasing its nutritional benefits.

Several theories by historians converge on the idea that the discovery of beer is correlated with human beings becoming sedentary and their desire to form a community of collective farmers. The earliest cultivations of spelt and barley appeared in Mesopotamia — and not primarily for feeding people, but for making them tipsy! We toast this idea that the happy hour is older than we imagined. The first traces of grapevines and evidence of wine-making appeared in the same region, a few thousand years after beer. The Sumerians of Mesopotamia were therefore the world's first master brewers and vintners. During this time, Africans were savoring the delights of mead, made from a fermentation of water and honey. The raising of goats and cows, which was widespread in Europe, gave rise to an ideal method for preserving milk for months and even years: cheese. Toward the middle of the 18th century, almost four tons of sauerkraut in barrels saved the crew of British sea captain James Cook from scurvy. It allowed them to survive a record-breaking three-year sailing voyage around the world. For centuries, the Scandinavian people preserved their precious vegetable harvests through lactofermentation, which helped them survive tough winters and other prolonged periods when nothing grew. The bacteria, yeasts and other microorganisms naturally present in our environment are not just useful, they have contributed to the pleasure, health, survival and progress of mankind since its origins.

THE AGE OF CLEANLINESS
In North America, where pasteurization is enshrined, as well as in the majority of developed countries, the practice of fermentation has been gradually eroded. We live in the age of cleanliness, hair removal, daily showers, anti-wrinkle creams and antibacterial soap. This new reality has its advantages and also its disadvantages. We have a general phobia about bacteria. Even the word frightens us. We associate bacteria with filth, sickness, epidemics and invaders. And yet, these tiny single-cell creatures are our friends, protecting our immune systems, aiding digestion and keeping us alive! We are covered in thousands of bacteria, inside and out. Bacteria clean us, protect us from illness and simplify nutrients to help our bodies absorb them.

To improve bacteria's image, the food industry has coined a more attractive name, suggesting a modern discovery: "probiotics," derived from the Latin pro and the Greek bios, and meaning "favorable to life." This more restrained term has gained the respect of consumers. So if you feel revulsion when you read the word "bacteria" in this book, substitute the word "probiotic" in your mind — it has a much better brand image.

"DON'T EAT THAT, THERE'S SOMETHING FUNNY ABOUT IT!"
"Don't eat that, it's gone bad!" We have all been lectured this way about a food at one time or another. Perhaps it was a slice of ham that had been unwrapped the week before, or a tub of hummus that had spent the afternoon in the sun. We may have picked up the hummus, examined it, sniffed it...and thought about what it had cost. Maybe it passed the sniff test and visual inspection — but then maybe a little tingle on the tongue during the taste test redirected it to the dog bowl or compost bin.

The ability to detect undesirable fermentation and rancid food is one of our oldest and most important instincts. There are very few innate reactions as powerful as the one we have when the odor of tainted meat hits our nostrils.

The power of this reaction has helped our species survive. Over the course of history, curiosity and famine have led human beings to sample foods that no longer had their original appearance, odor or texture, yet were not unpleasant. This happily opened the door to a world of new flavors and possibilities!

Fermentation is a culinary adventure that involves experimenting with the unknown, challenging preconceived notions and forcing one to rely on instinct. This type of experimentation encourages self-expression and rewards us with new flavors. Our first taste tests involving cheese, beer, whisky and wine are hardly ever "love at first bite" (or sip). Our taste for something develops as we become accustomed to its flavor. Once we accept a new flavor, it rewards us with a bouquet of subtle and heady aromas. With a food industry as sterilized and standardized as that of the Western world, the sense of adventure in sampling the new and unusual has atrophied. It has been replaced by insecurity, especially with regard to fermentations that move, change, expand, make bubbles and grow a coat of filaments. Fermented foods may look strange to us, but they also arouse our curiosity. We sniff a little, taste with the tip of our tongue, and then gradually suspicion gives way to a sense of privilege in eating a "living" food. The key to accepting: dare to taste! Take the time to familiarize yourselves with flavors and textures — then taste again!

THE MASON JAR FARMER

When we first take up fermenting, we become farmers in a way. We cultivate life and care for our "herd" of microorganisms. Like a farmer who watches over his cows, we watch over our living jars. Like a farmer, we are attentive to signs from our creatures — if they seem hungry or cold, or if they are suffering in an environment where there is too much light or oxygen. The good news is that making your own fermentations is even easier than taking care of a Tamagotchi, not to mention that the little attentions you give your creatures will reward you a hundred times over. Here are a few reasons to become a fermentation farmer that we think will inspire you:

Preserving

Most importantly, fermenting foods allows us to preserve them for a long time. It is actually possible to extend the shelf life of vegetables 50 times as long by fermenting them.

Having an environmentally responsible approach

Fermenting foods means saying goodbye to food waste: all the excess fresh food we have gets fermented instead of going in the trash! We also conserve energy by avoiding the cooking required for traditional preserves. We reduce the energy and resources required for the transformation, packaging and transportation of industrial products. Finally, doing our own fermentation allows us to choose the origin of our products and favor local foods over those that have traveled across two continents and used three modes of transportation before landing in the supermarket.

Saving money

By purchasing fruits and vegetables in season, while they are available in enormous quantities, we buy them at their lowest price. By fermenting them in different ways during harvest time, we save an unbelievable amount of money on our grocery bills. What's more, we can take advantage of many simple and economical foods, like cabbage, root vegetables, sugar, fruits and grains. After being transformed, these foods become more flavorful and exotic, thereby increasing their value. Because these ancient methods of preservation use so little energy, they yield an impressive return on a minimal investment. The only resource that's necessary is, most often, labor, and that's your best excuse to invite friends and family to help! That's what we make a habit of doing on sauerkraut and lactofermentation days: we gather together to work, discuss, sing...and once we're done, everyone leaves with their share of inexpensive treats and the memory of good stories told over a nice bottle of wine.

THE FIRST TIME...

As explorers in fermentation, we often begin an experiment whose end product is a mystery to us. Despite following directions, reading descriptions and recalling anecdotes, we know from experience that it is impossible to visualize a fermentation before it is right in front of us. This was especially true for a Japanese fermentation made from soybeans, called natto.

Seb had ordered bacteria on the Internet and received a miniature 2-teaspoon (10 mL) package, along with the tiniest spoon we could have imagined, about the size of a pin; $\frac{1}{100}$ of a teaspoon of fine white powder — that was the quantity to add to 2 pounds (1 kg) of cooked soybeans. We prepared everything in Sébastien's laundry room, which had been turned into a temperate fermentation lab for the occasion.

When Sébastien opened the door to his apartment after his workday, he was struck by the scent in the air. Not surprisingly, the scent grew stronger as he got closer to the laundry room. The verdict, after examining the fermentation mixture: totally extraterrestrial. The beans were covered in a fine, glossy substance the color of peanut butter. To date, it is the gluiest, most slippery substance we have ever encountered. Picture puffed rice and marshmallow squares that are still warm, that you can pull to infinity, with the marshmallow filaments stretching as thin as hairs without breaking.

The time had come to taste it. Instinctively, those who were faint of heart abstained...The texture was phenomenal, as slippery and rich as the best panna cotta you could imagine. The flavor was a little bland, but not bad. It was a success!

After some research, we discovered that the substance that gives natto its unique texture is called polyglutamic acid, and that natto contains nattokinase, an ingredient that some researchers have shown to be useful in the prevention of Alzheimer's disease and the treatment of cardiovascular disease. Natto also contains GABA (gamma-aminobutyric acid). This amino acid is the main neurotransmitter for calming nervous activity in the brain. GABA is used as a supplement to reduce stress and anxiety, improve mood and combat insomnia. Wow! We just created natural Prozac!

Cultivating Health

10 billion **bacteria** colonize the mouth.

1,000 billion bacteria *colonize the skin.*

10,000 billion bacteria inhabit the gut.

The body contains 10 times more bacteria than human cells.

IMAGINING ALL OF THIS BACTERIA MOVING ABOUT, inside the body and on its surface, is rather surreal. It's probably for the best that we can't observe it with the naked eye. The idea is enough to make us squirm, or even believe that our body doesn't belong to us! The fact is, we all live in symbiosis — dependent on one another but never consciously meeting up in our daily life. When we eat fermented foods, many of the useful microorganisms these foods contain settle in the digestive system. They concentrate in the large intestine, where they fulfill a number of missions:

- *They enhance the nutritional value of foods.* Unlike traditional preserves, where prolonged cooking tends to reduce the amount of nutrients in foods, including vitamin C (sorry, Grandma!), fermentation not only preserves but enhances the value of foods by increasing their nutritional content, for example of vitamin B_{12} or antioxidants. This is what happens with cabbage. Transformed into sauerkraut, its vitamin C content can soar by 400%!

- *They make foods more digestible.* Without the help of bacteria, many proteins, complex carbohydrates and vitamins would reach the end of the digestive tract still "undigested"; that is to say, the molecules would not have broken down sufficiently during the digestive process. They would remain too complex to pass through the intestinal membrane and then be absorbed by the body. In scientific terms, fermentation improves the bioavailability of nutrients. This means that the bacteria break down the foods until they are in a form that can be assimilated by the gut — and this action is essential! Once milk is fermented, it becomes more digestible because its lactose content has been reduced. That is why yogurt and kefir are more easily tolerated by individuals who are lactose-sensitive.

- *They contribute to the synthesis of certain vitamins.* Some bacteria are essential to the production of vitamins from other substances. This is the case with some forms of vitamins B and K.

- *They protect the system from invaders.* The "good" bacteria living in the gut prevent the proliferation of harmful bacteria or viruses, simply by monopolizing the space and resources that are available. They also have the ability to regulate the immune system, stimulating it when it is weakened and controlling it when it is overstimulated, for example in the case of allergy or inflammation.

- *In short, they make the job easier for us!* Getting more with less effort — we all have a lazy side, and fermentation fuels this hidden vice. Why struggle to expend our energy digesting food when bacteria can do it for us, improving its flavor and our health at the same time?

In our opinion, all these reasons are ample justification for starting a little revolution in the pantry!

BESIDES MAKING BUBBLES, HOW DOES FERMENTATION WORK?

Fermentation is based on the fundamental principles of life on earth: every form of life seeks a hospitable environment in which to live, defends itself to keep invaders away and rejects waste to maintain its balance. Without this cycle, no living thing could survive, no matter how gigantic or microscopic in size. Food fermentations are nothing more than the result of the survival cycle of a quantity of microorganisms that wander in search of nourishment. In many of these fermentations, sugar is the main food that is consumed by microorganisms, while lactic acid, acetic acid, alcohol and carbon dioxide are the main waste materials. These rejected substances are harmless to colonizing microorganisms, but make the environment inhospitable to the bacteria and yeasts that may be competing with them.

Yes, you have understood us correctly: it is the waste material of microorganisms that interests us. The digestive process of microorganisms produces a range of new molecules

LIFE-SAVING MOLD
Few people know that the first antibiotic, penicillin, was created not by man but by the mold *Penicillium*! Once cultivated and isolated by human beings, this toxin, lethal to many bacteria but harmless to the mold that produces it (luckily for our species!), has saved millions of lives.

called secondary metabolites. These make the flavor of a fermented food much more complex — and that's where the true magic of fermentation lies. Wine is one of the finest examples of this. And even though alcohol is the main product that comes from fermenting grapes, we rarely mention it when we sample a wine. Instead, we use olfactory images to describe the subtle flavors produced by fermentation: leather notes for Merlot, grapefruit for Sauvignon, vanilla for Burgundy, apricot for Chenin, hazelnut for Chardonnay, and so on. Often nonexistent in fresh grapes, these flavors are produced during fermentation and are created by different yeasts particular to their regions.

Wine is probably the most glamorous fermented product in the world. Following the same procedure, a simple sauerkraut fermented for three months will have a much more complex flavor than a cabbage marinated in vinegar for a few hours. The range of flavors created for the same food is influenced by the type and complexity of the communities of microorganisms that are present. It is also influenced by a variety of environmental factors, including temperature and the type of product being fermented.

BACTERIA, YEASTS AND MOLDS: SINGLE-CELLED CREATURES AT WORK!

As their name suggests, microorganisms are microscopic in size. Every mouthful of air we breathe contains yeasts, mold spores and bacteria, and the makeup of the organisms suspended in the air varies from one region to another. These wild microorganisms often contribute to the development of the characteristic flavor and even the types of fermentation that are possible in a given region. For example, the yellow wine of the Jura develops the flavor of sotolon (maple syrup), which is attributable to *Saccharomyces bayanus*, a type of yeast indigenous to the region. The banana notes sometimes identified in wheat beer, which are due to esters, are also produced by particular yeasts.

In many cases, bacteria, yeasts and molds work together, with the molds often playing a secondary role. The flavor of Camembert, for example, is mainly attributable to bacteria, but its bloomy rind, delicate flavors and runny texture are a result of molds. Much more fragile than bacteria and yeasts, molds proliferate only under very specific and stable conditions and in a humid and poorly ventilated environment — such as a bag of sliced bread forgotten on the counter. Left to grow in a propitious environment, these microscopic fungi create multicellular networks that manifest themselves in ways that are visible to the naked eye.

FRIENDLY CONSTRUCTION SITE SEEKING WORKING MICROORGANISMS

Everything, absolutely everything, ferments. It's just that certain fermentations, such as compost, are not food. Have you ever put your hand in a pile of compost in the middle of winter, only to discover that the internal temperature was that of a jacuzzi? That's fermentation!

All foods are fermentable, in different forms and using many combinations of organisms. Certain pairings are more compatible and more

ABOUT MOLD...

"All right, I can handle sauerkraut, but I'm still not ready to let stuff turn moldy in my home!"

It's true that the idea of eating moldy food is not especially appetizing, but it's all a question of getting accustomed to it. After all, you know you really like that Camembert with the moldy rind...I mean *bloomy* rind, as well as that mold-marbled ... I mean *veined* Roquefort, right? Taking your first steps as someone who lives dangerously, you may contemplate a raw-milk cheese whose rind is astonishingly well developed after a few days on the kitchen counter under a glass bell. You may also contemplate a jar of sauerkraut and its thin layer of harmless mold that you scrape off before diving in with no further thought. What's important is to explore these uncharted territories at your own pace and to enjoy the sense of discovery!

delicious than others. Every microorganism has the ability to ferment a number of elements, but always possesses a distinct specialization, its own tools and a domain in which it is the uncontested champion. For every food there are one or more ideal microscopic partners that will transform it into a culinary masterpiece or a killer cocktail. The combination that is sought will employ one of these methods:

- *Spontaneous fermentation,* which is based on the action of wild ferments — microorganisms that are naturally present in the air or on foods. This is the optimistic method for fermenting foods! By creating a favorable environment for proliferation, we attract these microorganisms, which will come along to colonize the environment and reward us for opening the door.

- *Inoculated fermentation,* which is based on introducing a single (pure culture) or several (mixed culture) ferments cultivated in an environment favorable to their proliferation. The advantage of this process is that it stabilizes certain fermentations that are more sensitive to the environment and provides access to a wider variety of microorganism strains.
  - A mixed culture is the basis of many fermentations (lactofermentations, kombucha, kefir, etc.). See also "Mixed," page 31.
  - A pure culture is the basis of many "modernized" or industrialized fermentations (including beer, wine, tempeh, some cheeses and some yeast-based breads), yielding results that are easier to guarantee and therefore products that can be reproduced. This predictable side also makes it appealing to beginner fermenters.

The Importance of Environment

Fish don't live in the desert, elephants won't put up with subarctic blizzards without a protest, penguins aren't happy eating hay, and the wolf can't live in harmony with the hare. Just as with animals, different microorganisms are not at ease sharing the same environment or eating the same things. The fermenting chef must create the ideal environment for the targeted bacteria, yeast or mold to make it feel at home, exploiting its specialty, reducing its competition and helping it take control. In addition to the right food/microorganism combination, a spontaneous or inoculated food fermentation that is successful (one in which only the desirable microorganisms proliferate) is heavily dependent on the environment. Each jar is a planet, with its own atmosphere either supplied with oxygen or deprived of it, along with its own temperature variations, resources and distinct population. The characteristics and quantities of these components will define the ability of a microorganism to live there and the type of world it will be able to create.

Will it have the necessary resources and tools to build a world that is alcoholic, acidic, vinegary or sweet? Will it create a world that is putrefied and unfit for consumption or one that is delightfully delicious?

In a jar of preserved lemons, for example, the environment includes lemons, salted brine and a hermetically sealed, oxygen-free space. A microorganism that cannot tolerate salt or the absence of oxygen, even if it adores citrus fruit, cannot survive there. For lactic bacteria, the super-specialists in fermentation in environments that are salted and oxygen-free, this environment is one of the most comfortable. Lactobacteria possess all the tools necessary (enzymes) to digest the available resources (sugar from the lemons). They discard substances (mainly lactic acid) that are beneficial or harmless to humans and they help preserve food. We would be crazy not to take advantage of our ability to create an environment in which they will proliferate, for example by maintaining a comfortable temperature. Faced with such hospitality, the useful microorganisms will inevitably settle in, have many children and live happily ever after! In short, to ferment is to spin a fairy tale for good little germs.

The Competition

A number of environmental factors ensure that the strain of ferment we want to see develop will easily overpower undesirable microorganisms. If it happens that two "enemy" strains are quarreling over the same lounge chair by the swimming pool, it may be better to take a few extra precautions to ensure that our VIP bacteria are not being intimidated.

Before you begin a fermentation, your containers, instruments, work surfaces and hands(!) must be carefully washed and rinsed to limit the presence of undesirable microorganisms. We are not maniacs when it comes to sterilization, simply because sterilization is not often required. Acidic or mixed fermentations (lactofermentations of vegetables, kombucha, kefir, vinegars, etc.) are robust and often sufficiently ferocious to prevent invaders from taking control. A thorough washing suffices. Milk-based fermentations are fairly robust. It is probably wise to sanitize your containers and instruments the first time. After a few experiments with your equipment, you can simply wash them. For more delicate fermentations, like alcoholic liquids (beer, sake, root beer, mead, etc.), sanitizing is a must.

CLEANING METHODS

Washing: Wash with dish detergent and hot water, then rinse carefully with fresh water.

Sanitizing: Rinse with a solution of 1 tbsp (15 mL) liquid bleach in 16 cups (4 L) water for 30 seconds, then rinse carefully with fresh water. Always wash equipment before sanitizing it!

If you follow the suggested sanitizing method, spores or microorganisms will remain, but in insufficient quantities to contaminate the fermentation. Sanitizing products for brewers can also be used. Sanitization by scalding or by spraying with 70% alcohol is not advised. Boiling water can crack glass jars, and the alcohol that is sold as a disinfectant at the drugstore often contains bittering agents. Without proper rinsing, these agents may end up in your foods.

SUGAR, PROTEIN AND FRESH WATER

The end product of fermentation will naturally depend on the colonizing microorganisms. It will also depend on the food the microorganisms have access to. Like human beings, microorganisms get their energy from one of three nutrients: carbohydrates (sugars), proteins and, less frequently, lipids (fats).

Carbohydrates (Sugars)

Sugar is the principle fuel for life on earth and is found in one form or another in most of the living elements that surround us. Sugars are the easiest, most useful and most efficient nutrients to ferment. Sugar in one form or another is the source of miraculous food products from beer and bread to cider, yogurt and kombucha.

Carbohydrates can arrange themselves in longer or shorter chains, forming different types of sugars that are fairly easy to ferment. The more complex the sugars, the less sweet they taste and the more specialized the microorganisms required to transform them into simple sugars. A fruit contains a lot of simple sugars (fructose and glucose). Thanks to the multitude of wild bacteria, yeasts and molds in the air or on its skin, it will ferment without any help. This is called spontaneous fermentation.

The champions in the consumption of simple sugars are yeasts; they generally transform sugars into alcohol. If the sugar becomes complex and forms long chains — for example, the starch in rice — it is necessary to add a specific mold, such as koji, to eventually turn it into sake. This is called inoculated fermentation. The mold produces an enzyme called amylase, whose precise role is to simplify the starch but not the other complex carbohydrates.

Proteins

Although proteins are less frequently targeted in food fermentation, they are subject to fermentation and produce very interesting results. The amount of protein absorbed when we eat tempeh is much higher than if we eat the same quantity of unfermented soy, because the proteins in tempeh have been simplified and some of the proteins that prevent the digestion of soy have been rendered inactive.

Mold is the champion when it comes to fermenting proteins. The whitish substance on the surface of dried sausage and cheese is a good example of friendly mold that simplifies proteins and fats, creating complex flavors and helping prevent oxidation. In Camembert, the breaking down of proteins by mold is what makes the cheese runny.

Water

Water itself is not a source of energy, but it is still a vital ingredient in all fermentation of microorganisms. Dehydration is an effective process for preserving food because it removes the water from the food. The more water there is in a food, the more easily bacteria settle in. Water content can be expressed as a percentage of total weight. For example, milk (87% water), brine (typically 98% water and 2% salt) and the vegetables we add to brine are species suited to fermentation using lactobacteria. Sweetened liquids, which are lower in water content and higher in sugar content (grape juice can contain 12% sugar, therefore 88% water), are favorable to the development of yeasts and bacteria; yeasts, however, tend to take control more quickly. Bread (about 30% water), which is lower in water content and has no wet surface, is favorable to the development of mold but not bacteria. That is why bread can be kept at room temperature without spoiling.

Our recipes that call for adding water will work with the water in any country, even water of questionable quality, but your choice of water will influence the flavor of the finished product.

- *Tap water (filtered):* Tap water is acceptable for fermentations. Its mineral content is high (which is desirable). Unfortunately, tap water also contains a small amount of chlorine and other ugly stuff that doesn't taste very good. We recommend using a simple active charcoal filter to eliminate chlorine, reduce other undesirable compounds and improve the taste of the water overall. Allowing the water to "breathe" for 12 hours on the counter also helps eliminate chlorine. If your water is very hard (for example, if you live within a few miles/kilometers from the sea), an inverse osmosis filtration system may prove useful.

- *Spring water:* Spring water costs more, and obtaining it is more complicated, but if you want your end product to be of the highest quality, using the best water may make a difference. There isn't a marked contrast when it comes to lactofermented vegetables or fruits, but there is a big difference when it comes to products that are essentially water-based, including kombucha, water kefir and beer.

- *Distilled and reverse-osmosis water:* Distilled water is not recommended for fermentations because it has been stripped of minerals. Minerals improve the effectiveness of extractions and infusions. Most importantly, we need minerals to survive! Minerals are as good for microorganisms as they are for us. The absence of minerals compromises the growth of microorganisms and may hinder the fermentation process. Too many minerals, on the other hand, may also impede the process. Using a reverse-osmosis system, it is possible to adjust the quantity of minerals extracted, which is measured in total ppm (parts per million). The general consensus is that a mineral content of about 150 ppm is ideal.

The different types of fermentation

ALCOHOLIC

Ferment: Pure yeast cultures (in packets or vials) or wild yeasts found on the peels, shells, pods and hulls of foods or in the air.

Environment: 60°F (16°C) for slow fermentations (cider, wine), from 68°F to 71.5°F (20°C to 22°C) for slightly quicker fermentations (beer) and from 95°F (35°C) for quick fermentations (bread); in a sanitized container, except for quick fermentations.

The uncontested masters in the making of alcohol are yeasts. Alcoholic fermentation produces beer, wine, cider, sake, whisky — even bread! Using the sugars in the flour, yeasts are responsible for the formation of bubbles in the dough and the particular aromas in bread that people have loved from time immemorial. Yeasts consume sugars and discard half as alcohol and half as carbon dioxide. So if a solution contains 10% sugar to start, the liquid at the end, after fermentation is complete, will have an alcohol content of about 5%. Alcoholic fermentation is an effective means of preservation because it has a toxic effect on other microorganisms, thus protecting the product from transformation by these microorganisms.

Alcoholic fermentations either require the addition of a ferment (such as our favorite champagne yeast, EC-1118) or depend on wild yeasts that are attracted by sweet bait. Because the basic rule of alcoholic fermentation is to maintain an environment that is deprived of oxygen (anaerobic), this type of fermentation must take place in an airtight container equipped with an airlock (see page 32). An airlock allows the evacuation of the large quantity of carbon dioxide that is produced, while preventing oxygen from entering.

DEMYSTIFYING LATIN AND GREEK

Don't be intimidated by the complex words of Latin or Greek origin on the packaging of fermented products. They often define things that are actually fairly simple.

Schizosaccharomyces may not sound very appetizing, until you take the mystery out of it: *schizo* from the Greek "to divide"; *saccharo*, Greco-Latin for "sugar"; and *myces*, for "fungi." Therefore: fungi that divide themselves (by feeding) on sugar.

It's the same for *Lactobacillus cremoris*: *lacto,* from the Latin for "milk"; *bacillus,* "in the shape of a small stick"; and *cremoris*, "having the appearance of cream." Therefore: (organisms) in milk that have the shape of small sticks and look like cream. In other words: yogurt cultures!

LACTIC

Ferment: Lactic bacteria in pure or mixed form for inoculated fermentation (packets for yogurt, kefir grains); wild bacteria for the spontaneous fermentation of most vegetables.

Environment: Sugar present; aqueous.
- Vegetables: Salted (brine containing 1% salt or more); oxygen absent (to prevent mold from developing); temperatures from 59°F to 77°F (15°C to 25°C); in a washed container.

- Milks (ideally pasteurized, for safety reasons): Oxygen present or absent; temperatures from 64.5°F to 82.5°F (18°C to 28°C) for kefir or from 95°F to 107.5°F (35°C to 42°C) for yogurt and most cheeses; in a sanitized container.

Lactic bacteria are a large family of organisms responsible for many simple and delicious milk-based fermentations (yogurt, kefir, cheese). They are also responsible for the fermentation in salted products (sauerkraut, kimchi, pickles, capers, miso, dry sausage). Lactobacteria feed on sugars and discard lactic acid, which quickly acidifies the environment.

Lactic bacteria are very robust. It is therefore possible to use the bacteria naturally present in the environment simply by attracting them with the right parameters. Sauerkraut and kimchi, for example, do not need a strain of bacteria imposed on them; they transform on their own, naturally and quickly! The lactic bacteria that live on vegetables have no competition in a briny environment deprived of oxygen.

SO IS SALT GOOD OR NOT?

"Table" salt is fine for deicing roads in winter, but from a nutritional standpoint it's not that great. On the other hand, sea salt, pink Himalayan salt and fleur de sel harvested by hand are good choices! Sea salt, for example, contains more than 70 minerals, whereas table salt contains only sodium chloride (with added anticaking agents, a touch of iodine and, very often, sugar). Sea salt is marvelous for improving our absorption of water, helping the nervous system function properly and maintaining the fluid balance in our cells. Best of all, it helps us turn vegetables into something a lot more interesting!

Cow's milk contains about 5% lactose (a molecule of glucose attached to a molecule of galactose). Lactose is a sugar that few mammals can digest well, including most human beings over the age of five. Introduced into such an environment, lactobacteria will feed on the lactose and quickly take control over the environment, diminishing the amount of lactose and producing lactic acid in sufficient quantities to acidify the environment. This makes the environment intolerable to other bacteria, molds or yeasts, including harmful bacteria.

Lactic fermentations that are not carried out in a very salty, anaerobic environment benefit from being started with cultivated bacteria, to give them more stability. Lactic bacteria cultures are often interchangeable, so if you want to make cheese from nuts, you can use a little yogurt, a packet of freeze-dried bacteria, a small spoonful of miso, a little active sauerkraut juice or even water kefir grains. Lactic cultures are the most common fermented foods; you likely have at least two or three in your refrigerator right now.

ACETIC

Ferment: Acetic bacteria, always wild, in spontaneous or inoculated fermentation from another strain of active wild bacteria (kombucha, apple cider vinegar).

Environment: Aqueous; alcohol present; oxygen present; temperature from 59°F to 95°F (15°C to 35°C); in a washed container.

The word "acetic" derives from the Latin *aceto*, meaning "vinegar." The role of acetic bacteria is to transform alcohol into acetic acid, which gives vinegar its distinctive flavor. At first glance, the roles of acetic acid and lactic acid may seem similar, but vinegar has a much sharper acidic flavor and a strong odor, while lactic acid is sweeter and odorless.

Acetic fermentation is always of second order: it takes place in an environment that has first been fermented by yeasts — that is, in alcoholic products. While alcoholic fermentation is a less effective means of preserving food, it requires an oxygen-deprived environment, and acetic bacteria not only tolerate alcohol but thrive in such an environment. Moreover, they jump for joy when the container is no longer airtight and the wine, beer, cider or any other alcoholic product comes into contact with oxygen. Fed by oxygen, the acetic bacteria can then digest the alcohol as if it were sugar.

Kombucha is an excellent example of fermentation in which yeasts and bacteria work together. While the yeasts are producing alcohol, the acetic bacteria transform it into acetic acid, as if they were working in a production line. This explains why kombucha has a very low alcohol content and a slightly vinegary flavor.

Preserving foods using acetic acid (added vinegar), commonly known as marinating, has become a substitute for lactic fermentation because it is faster and easier. Although marinating plays an important role in food production, it does not produce the wide range of complex flavors that lactic fermentation does.

AMYLOLYTIC

Ferment: Molds.

Environment: High starch content; oxygen present; moist or humid; variable temperature between 71.5°F and 95°F (22°C and 35°C); in a washed container.

An amylolytic fermentation (from the Greek *amylo*, for "starch," and *lytic*, "that which cuts") is produced when certain molds develop on a product composed mainly of starch. The molds secrete an enzyme called amylase, which cuts the starch in long-chain sugars into simpler sugars. The result is a sweet product that can be easily digested by these molds or by other microorganisms, such as yeasts.

These fermentations are not very well known in the Western world because of the high temperature and humidity required for them to grow. They are more popular in Asia, where the mold *Aspergillus oryzae* is cultivated to make koji and nuruk, which to some extent replace the malt used in North America and Europe. Given the high starch content in starchy foods, it is possible to transform a soup of cooked rice into a sweet syrup in just 24 hours by adding a few spoonfuls of koji, thanks to the amylase secreted by these molds. This syrup is then used for the alcoholic fermentation of sake.

Amylolytic fermentation is most often used as an intermediary to simplify sugars before they are fermented to produce alcohol. Industries follow this enzymatic procedure to make corn syrup and rice syrup. The same process takes place in your mouth each time you eat starchy food, because your saliva contains the amylase needed to simplify the complex carbohydrates.

PROTEOLYTIC

Ferment: Mainly molds, ferments that are pure and controlled in the form of packets.

Environment: High protein content; humid, but not wet; temperature from 82.5°F to 93°F (28°C to 34°C); in a washed container.

You will have guessed that this type of fermentation involves proteins. The fermentation is made possible by protease, an enzyme secreted in large quantities by molds. A good example of proteolytic fermentation is tempeh, a fermentation of soybeans that comes from Indonesia and is often referred to as the ancestor of tofu. The mold *Rhizopus oligosporus* or the mold *Rhizopus oryzae* develops on soybeans while "soldering" them together into a kind of pancake. The protease released by the mold simplifies certain proteins and renders them more easily absorbed.

Another well-known proteolytic fermentation that is observed as much in medicine as it is in bread is the mold *Penicillium*, which grows on the rinds of soft cheeses and digests the proteins that make the cheeses firm. Over time, the cheeses develop richer flavors, and their texture becomes runnier.

MIXED

Ferment: Strong cultures that are better in their natural form (sourdough, kefir grains, liquid kombucha) than in industrial form (powder, bricks). It is often easy to find these traditional ferments in the homes of individuals in our community; it is also a good occasion to talk about mold with someone who understands us!

Environments: Generally sweet; oxygen present or absent; various stable temperatures; no direct sunlight (which can make the temperature vary); usually in a washed container.

A mixed fermentation occurs when two or more types of microorganisms act in symbiosis to transform their environment. Because two are stronger than one, they make the most robust fermentations. Water kefir, kombucha and cheese with a bloomy rind are a few examples.

In general, the two types of fermentation follow one after another in a well-synchronized dance. In kombucha, the yeasts first transform the sugar into alcohol, which then prompts the acetic bacteria to transform the alcohol into vinegar. In water kefir, alcoholic and lactic fermentations work together to make a product that reaches maturity in just 48 hours.

Other mixed fermentations are caused by a greater change in environment. In the case of cheese, the milk is fermented with lactic bacteria to acidify it, causing the milk to curdle. Next, the curdled milk is pressed and salt is added to obtain a solid that is rich in protein and contains much less lactose and water than milk. Molds and certain bacteria that can tolerate salt then form on the rind of the cheese and "digest" the interior, causing it to develop a variety of flavors and textures.

OLD SOCKS FOR SUPPER?
The bacteria *Brevibacterium linens,* which are responsible for the strong odor of Muenster, limburger and the raclette that makes you salivate, are actually the same bacteria that cause foot odor...which just goes to show that taste is a matter of perspective!

Useful Equipment

1. JARS

We secretly worship John Landis Mason, the inventor of the mason jar. These containers are suitable for all recipes; we can boil them, chill them, adjust the lids and even drop them! They can usually stand in for more high-tech equipment sold at five times the price. Always make sure the lids and rings are not damaged or corroded. Jars with a rubber gasket and glass lid, along with food-grade ceramic, stoneware and stainless steel containers, are good choices. PET food-grade plastic will do the job, but isn't as pretty. Metals other than stainless steel should not come into direct contact with your fermentation, because they will corrode.

2. FINE-WEAVE FABRIC AND NUT MILK BAGS

Nylon washes out more easily; cotton filters better. We have our internal debates: David is a purist and prefers cotton, while Sébastien likes to save time and prefers nylon. You'll have to choose your camp.

3. CARBOY OR FERMENTATION JUG

Usually made of glass, this jug has a small mouth, which makes it more practical for the fermentation of alcoholized liquids.

4. AIRLOCK

This simple plastic gadget, which costs next to nothing, will make you feel like a pro. Attached to the lid of a jar or bucket, or to the cork of a fermentation jug, this little tool allows gases to escape and prevents the buildup of excess pressure in a sealed container. At the same time, it keeps air, oxygen and insects out. There is a wide range of new models on the market: waterless, with an integrated weight, cruelty-free, gluten-free, etc. They are all good, so explore the options!

5. WEIGHTS

Weights are essential in brine fermentations to keep foods submerged. Many kinds of weights are available on the market, but there's nothing to prevent you from using your creativity. A weight could be the well-trimmed core of a cabbage, a thick slice of daikon radish, a small plate, an espresso cup or even a freezer bag filled with pebbles or water!

2. FINE-WEAVE FABRIC
AND NUT MILK BAGS

4. AIRLOCK

3. CARBOY OR
FERMENTATION JUG

1. JARS

5. WEIGHTS

11. BOWLS

9. THERMOCIRCULATOR
(SOUS VIDE IMMERSION
CIRCULATOR)

8. INCUBATOR

CAUTION
HOT SURFACE

7. HEAT REGULATOR

nutrichef™

A419

10. KETTLE

6. KITCHEN SCALE

12. CHEESECLOTH

6. KITCHEN SCALE

The standard digital kitchen scale, which has a precision of +/– 0.2 oz (5 g) and a capacity of 4 to 11 lbs (2 to 5 kg), is very useful for home fermentation. It allows you to measure the weight of a 2- or 4-lb (1 or 2 kg) cabbage. The margin of error for measurements in fermentation is about 5%. Therefore, if a recipe calls for 2 lbs 3 oz (1 kg) of sugar, using between 2 lbs 1 oz and 2 lbs 5 oz (950 g and 1.05 kg) is acceptable and will not have an impact on the final product.

7. HEAT REGULATOR

This temperature controller can be connected to any refrigerator or incubator. For example, it can be connected to the fridge to keep the temperature cooler in summer for making sauerkraut, or connected to a lamp in an enclosed space to make koji.

8. INCUBATOR

An incubator is an enclosed space in which the temperature is controlled to maintain an ideal environment. In many cases, this corresponds to a temperature higher than room temperature. There are professional incubators, but for home fermentation, it is often sufficient to find a warmer area in your home. One example: the oven of an electric range, with the heat off and the oven light on (the temperature generally hovers around 90°F/32°C). Another example: a cooler in which you place jars of very hot water. To check the temperature inside without opening the incubator and letting the heat escape, use an electronic thermometer with a probe (install the probe inside and place the digital screen outside). If you opt for the oven, be careful to put a sign on the range so your roommate who has a sudden craving for pizza won't be responsible for the unpremeditated murder of your fermentation!

9. THERMOCIRCULATOR (SOUS VIDE IMMERSION CIRCULATOR)

This is a stick equipped with a heating element and thermostat that can be placed in any large container filled with water. Once the water reaches the desired temperature, you can set your jars in the container to make yogurt, or place everything in an enclosed space to make it an incubator. Thermocirculators designed for home use are not too expensive and can be useful for cooking all kinds of dishes (like the perfect soft-boiled egg or sous vide vegetables).

10. KETTLE

When we start fermenting, we need to be able to boil water to make infusions and to sanitize tools, among other things. For the purposes of this book, an 8-cup (2 L) kettle will suffice.

11. BOWLS

Two large stainless steel mixing bowls or round-bottomed bowls will be perfect for mixing ingredients. Stainless steel is easier to clean and doesn't get scratched as easily as plastic, which means there will be fewer hiding places for unfavorable bacteria to grow. On a practical level, stainless steel and plastic are the same.

12. CHEESECLOTH

A classic that hasn't lost its usefulness in the kitchen. For labneh, it's all you will need. Seriously!

13. PLASTIC BUCKETS

Here, the size you choose — 1, 2½ or 5 gallons (4, 10 or 20 L) — will generally dictate the size of your fermentation and at the same time attest to your level of confidence. Choose no. 2 food-grade plastic, preferably PET or HDPET, as these are the safest plastics. We prefer reused buckets, as long as the plastic is not discolored or damaged and the buckets did not contain toxic or inedible products. Plastic buckets can also serve as carboys.

Because they can be even better

THERE'S NOTHING BETTER THAN VEGETABLES for your first experiments with cultures in jars. Vegetables are stable, versatile and almost impossible to ruin. Well, actually, you can ruin them, but if you follow our advice, it won't happen as often. Be sure to use fresh vegetables with no trace of mold on them.

HOW DO I KNOW IF A VEGETABLE CAN BE FERMENTED?

If it contains water and sugar (therefore, if it is a vegetable!), it can ferment. Having said that, potatoes are a delicate matter and we don't recommend them for novices. The same goes for Brussels sprouts, which are cute but develop an overpowering odor once they are fermented. Since all vegetables are subject to lactofermentation (see also page 28), lactic acid bacteria win the popularity prize in this chapter.

THE 2% RULE

Salt creates an environment that promotes the growth of lactic acid bacteria while discouraging the development of undesirable microorganisms. For the majority of lactofermented vegetables, the sacrosanct rule is for the proportion of salt to equal 2% of the total weight of the ingredients. Root vegetables, which contain less water and less indigenous bacteria (especially if they have been peeled), as well as sweeter vegetables (like beets), will benefit from an additional source of lactic acid bacteria. The source can be the liquid from another active (unpasteurized) lactofermentation (like sauerkraut, kimchi or pickles) or lactic acid starter culture powder, which you can find in the yogurt section of your natural foods store. Other lactofermentations, including spicy sauces, olives, umeboshi plums and cheeses, require higher percentages of salt. Use the chart on page 38 to help you calculate the amount of salt you will need according to the food being fermented.

BRINING CHART FOR LACTOFERMENTATIONS

Brine Amount of salt per 2 lb 3 oz/1 kg	2% 4 tsp (20 g) salt per 2 lb 3 oz (1 kg)	4% 8 tsp (40 g) salt per 2 lb 3 oz (1 kg)		10% 20 tsp (100 g) salt per 2 lb 3 oz (1 kg)
	All vegetables not appearing on this chart (except potatoes and Brussels sprouts)	Pickles	Beets	Olives
		Chile peppers and spicy sauces	Jerusalem artichokes	Umeboshi plums
	Citrus fruit	Citrus fruit	Squash	

The total weight corresponds to the combined weight of the food and the water (if applicable).

The liquid in active sauerkraut (or another unpasteurized vegetable lactofermentation) is a practical source of lactobacteria. You can also use one-quarter of a 5-gram packet of lactic acid starter culture powder.

CANNING IN JARS AND JAR BURPING TECHNIQUE

For all lactofermentation in jars, carbon dioxide must be allowed to escape from the container (especially for the first 2 days), but air must be kept out. Oxygen is the enemy to avoid, because its presence causes browning and allows mold to proliferate. Note: it is not necessary to sanitize the jars and instruments — a thorough washing will suffice.

1. Fill the jar almost to full capacity, just to the base of the neck; the more air you leave under the lid, the greater the risk of contact with oxygen.
2. Compress food carefully (using your hands or a pounder) to ensure that no air bubbles remain under the surface.
3. Cover with a cabbage leaf (ideally), to contain stray bits of food.
4. Place one or more weights on the leaf, enough to keep food submerged.
5. If needed, cover food in more brine (see chart) to keep it from coming into contact with air.
6. If you are serious, meticulous and a bit of a control freak, you will have your airlocks ready at hand, but if you are calm and confident enough, you can use the following technique:

- For jars from store-bought foods that you have reused, set the lid on top of the jar, without screwing it on, then place a weight on top.
- For mason jars, place the lid on top and turn the ring with your fingertips without sealing the jar completely.
- For jars with a rubber gasket and hinged lid, close by using the spring lock.

7. To prevent spills, stand the jar in another container to collect liquid that may overflow.
8. Let ferment in the dark at 59°F to 77°F (15°C to 25°C), taking care to wipe the exterior of the jar the first few days in case of overflow; if necessary, once a day for the first 3 or 4 days, you can even use your fingers or a spoon to submerge vegetables that float to the top. As of the fifth day, do not open the jars until the minimum recommended number of days in the recipe has passed.
9. Once the fermentation is to your taste, place it in the refrigerator or a cold pantry. In a closed jar, it will often keep for up to 1 year, but it will also turn more acidic. Once the jar is opened, it will keep for a few weeks in the refrigerator.

HOW DO I KNOW WHEN IT'S READY?

It's not an exact science, due to the variability of the environment and personal preferences. The recommended times in the recipes have been calculated according to an ideal and stable temperature and to reflect popular taste. If your palate is sensitive to acidity, we recommend smelling and tasting the contents of your jars after the minimum recommended number of days in the recipe. If you like food that packs a punch, wait a few more days!

CAN I POISON MYSELF?

If you're the type of person who will eat foul-smelling food with a totally unacceptable appearance, you could poison yourself. The pH of a lactofermentation drops rapidly under 4.2 (the lower the pH, the more acidic the product). All of the microorganisms that could make you sick do not grow in such an environment. That's why the risk of poisoning is minimal, even nonexistent, as long as you have sound judgment. How to guarantee success? Avoid contact with oxygen in every possible way after the first 5 days and always keep the vegetables submerged. The longer you leave the vegetables to ferment without interfering, the more acidic the contents will be. Leaving them longer without interference also reduces the risk of the contents reacting to the oxygen when you finally open the jar.

Odor

A failed lactofermentation is the opposite of subtle. It smells like garbage. A successful fermentation smells like a marinade. It should not have a strong yeasty odor (although, if it does, it will still be edible).

Aspect

Moss, fur or filaments of any color are not desired in this chapter. With a little luck (and no oxygen), the surface of the food in your jar will remain nice and clean.

- If the liquid turns cloudy in the first few days, it's a sign that everything is fine! It will turn clear again in a few days. A whitish deposit may become visible at the bottom of the jars. This deposit is as inoffensive as the little white spots on vegetables.
- If your pickles are growing "fur," it's because oxygen has infiltrated and mold has proliferated. There are two schools of thought, one of which is "Throw it out." We believe, as do most people who are used to making fermentations, that it's totally fine to remove this top layer and save the rest of the vegetables that were submerged and not in contact with oxygen.
- If your vegetables have turned brown and look spoiled, they probably are! But keep in mind that there is always a change in color during fermentation. Pickles will go from light green to olive green; "red" cabbage will go from purple to pink, and so forth.
- In the very rare eventuality that molds of a fluorescent shade (yellow, violet or pink), black or forest green appear, or a gluey substance forms, it means the fermentation was not done correctly. Either discard it or save it as a display for next Halloween.
- Once the jar is open, a thin, brittle white layer (Kahm yeast) may develop on the surface of the brine, especially if the storage temperature was a little too high. It is completely inoffensive and can be consumed without a problem. To prevent it from developing, store the jar in the fridge once it has been opened.

The Ancestral Recipe

Sauerkraut is the classic of classics in fermentation. It is also a rite of passage for the fermenter apprentice. If, at first, the experiment seems too laborious, start over and practice until you've mastered it. Most of the other recipes will then seem a lot more accessible.

LEVEL OF DIFFICULTY

TYPE OF FERMENTATION
Lactic

PREPARATION TIME
20 minutes

FERMENTATION TIME
3 weeks

EQUIPMENT
Scale, mandoline or chef's knife, bowl, 1-quart (1 L) glass jar or fermentation jug, pounder (optional), weight (optional), airlock (optional)

2 lb 3 oz (1 kg) white and/or red cabbage

4 tsp (20 g) sea salt

1 tsp (5 mL) caraway seeds

1 tsp (5 mL) freshly ground black pepper

1 tsp (5 mL) spices that inspire you

Sauerkraut

1. Set aside 1 whole cabbage leaf. Using a mandoline or chef's knife, finely chop remaining cabbage and place in a bowl. Add salt, caraway seeds, black pepper and any other spices that inspire you.

2. Mix with your hands for a few minutes, until cabbage begins to release water. Some may find this a sensual experience...

3. Transfer to the jar or fermentation jug, in small quantities, pressing down cabbage each time by hand or using a pounder. The liquid that is produced should submerge the cabbage.

4. Place cabbage leaf on top of mixture to prevent cabbage bits from coming into contact with air. Place a weight on top of cabbage leaf if necessary to keep it submerged.

5. Use the jar burping technique (see page 38) or an airlock.

6. Let ferment out of direct light for 3 weeks.

7. Remove weight inside jar and discard bits of cabbage floating on the surface, if any. Taste sauerkraut, which should be acidic.

Spoon a generous portion on top of a Tempeh Burger (page 177) or use it as an accompaniment to just about anything else you eat.

Keeps for 1 year in the refrigerator.

TYPE OF FERMENTATION
Lactic

PREPARATION TIME
20 minutes

FERMENTATION TIME
3 to 5 weeks

EQUIPMENT
Scale, mandoline, bowl, 1-quart (1 L) glass jar or fermentation jug, pounder (optional), weight (optional), airlock (optional)

LACTOFERMENTED
Root Vegetables

18 OZ (500 G) TRIMMED ROOT VEGETABLES, FOR EXAMPLE:

1 lb (450 g) beets and 1¾ oz (50 g) garlic scapes

10½ oz (300 g) multicolored carrots, 5¼ oz (150 g) turnips and 1¾ oz (50 g) onions

18 oz (500 g) Jerusalem artichokes

9 oz (250 g) multicolored carrots and 9 oz (250 g) daikon radish

2 tsp (10 g) salt (or 2% of total weight of vegetables)

Your choice of herbs or aromatics — go wild!

¼ of a 5-g packet of lactic acid starter culture powder or 6 tbsp + 2 tsp (100 mL) sauerkraut juice (especially recommended if using Jerusalem artichokes or beets, optional for other vegetables)

1 whole cabbage leaf (optional)

2% BRINE (IF NEEDED)

4 tsp (20 g) salt

4 cups (1 L) water, at room temperature

1. Peel, cut, slice and shred vegetables until desired weight is obtained (total trimmed weight should be 18 oz/500 g). The size of the pieces is at your discretion.

2. In a bowl, using your hands, thoroughly mix vegetables, salt, herbs and starter culture (if using) for a few minutes. Let stand for about 10 minutes or until vegetables begin to release liquid.

3. Transfer to the jar or fermentation jug, in small quantities, pressing down mixture each time using your hands or a pounder.

4. If not enough liquid is produced by the vegetables to cover them, prepare 2% brine by dissolving salt in water, then pour enough into jar to cover vegetables.

5. Cover with a cabbage leaf or plastic food wrap and place a weight on top, if needed.

6. Use the jar burping technique (see page 38) or an airlock.

7. Let ferment out of direct light for 3 to 5 weeks.

Explore pairing these vegetables with different foods. Add them to a salad, sandwich or Dragon Bowl (page 161), or eat them alone with a fork.

Keeps for 1 year in the refrigerator and probably longer.

These are not complicated, they're pretty and they impress the ladies. All root vegetables work. On the other hand, because the sugar levels in these vegetables (especially beets) are higher than in cabbage, it is better to add sauerkraut juice or another source of lactic acid bacteria, such as starter culture, to prevent alcoholic fermentation. No, you don't always have to add this, but why take a chance? It's better for your self-esteem to make the first experiment a success.

In the outdoor markets of Kyoto, food stands sell all kinds of lactofermented vegetables made with miso or the solid leftovers of sake fermentation. In this recipe for misozuke, also known as tsukemono, the miso serves as solid brine for the vegetables. The major interest in this type of fermentation is that the vegetables do not need to be immersed in the brine; a coating suffices. And since slightly softened vegetables work very well in this recipe, it is a surprising way to use the forgotten specimens in your fridge before the call to compost becomes unavoidable... If you are the type of person who needs to work with precise amounts and times, don't venture into this recipe, because the rules are hazy. The more adventurous type will also be more inclined to appreciate the unfamiliar flavor of misozuke.

LEVEL OF DIFFICULTY

TYPE OF FERMENTATION
Lactic

PREPARATION TIME
10 minutes

FERMENTATION TIME
5 to 30 days

EQUIPMENT
Scale, bowl, shallow airtight plastic container with lid

Root Vegetables
IN MISO BRINE
(MISOZUKE OR TSUKEMONO)

MISO BRINE

18 oz (500 g) homemade Miso (page 148) or store-bought miso

1 cup (200 g) granulated sugar or 1 cup (250 mL) mirin

¼ cup (60 g) salt

2 tbsp (30 mL) grated gingerroot

1 tbsp (15 mL) Sake (page 143)

ROOT VEGETABLE MISOZUKE

14 oz (400 g) trimmed fresh root vegetables (for example, carrots, parsnips, radishes, daikon radishes), ideally slightly softened (see box, opposite)

8 tsp (40 mL) granulated sugar

4 tsp (20 g) salt

1. *Brine:* In a bowl, mix miso, sugar, salt, ginger and sake into a smooth, moist paste. Add a little water if needed.

2. *Misozuke:* Place whole root vegetables in a shallow plastic container and cover with miso brine, keeping vegetables from touching one another as much as possible. Cover with plastic food wrap directly on the surface to prevent miso from drying out, then seal the container with its lid.

3. Let ferment at room temperature for 5 to 30 days, according to desired "cooking" time. The larger the vegetable, the longer it will take to ferment. It will also take a little longer if the misozuke is stored in the refrigerator.

4. When ready to serve, wipe the brine off the vegetables and taste them! Save the brine.

5. Once all the vegetables have been eaten, add 8 tsp (40 mL) sugar and 4 tsp (20 g) salt to the misozuke mixture and refrigerate for future use (see below). It will keep up to 3 months.

Use the root vegetables in brine as an accompaniment to a rice dish or a Misozuke Roll (page 170). You can use the leftover brine as you would use miso.

Out of the brine, the vegetables will keep for 3 to 5 days in the refrigerator. In brine, always refrigerated, they will keep for 6 weeks.

TIP

It is also possible to make fish misozuke by replacing the vegetables with thin fillets of very fresh mackerel or snapper (or other white fish). Use a large resealable freezer bag and refrigerate fish in the brine for 24 to 36 hours before removing the brine and cooking the fish.

LEVEL OF DIFFICULTY

TYPE OF FERMENTATION
Lactic

PREPARATION TIME
30 minutes

FERMENTATION TIME
3 days to 3 weeks

EQUIPMENT
Scale, bowls, two 1-quart (1 L) glass jars, airlocks (optional)

Pickled CUCUMBERS

---

2 lbs 3 oz (1 kg) pickling cucumbers (new and crunchy is always better than old and wizened)

6 cups (1.5 L) cold water

3 cups (750 mL) ice cubes

5% SWEET BRINE

8 tsp (40 g) salt

1 tbsp (15 mL) granulated sugar

4 cups (1 L) water, at room temperature

2 grape leaves, fresh, new, frozen or lactofermented (see recipe, page 54) (optional)

2 cloves garlic

1 bunch fresh dill

1 tsp (5 mL) black peppercorns

1 tsp (5 mL) caraway seeds

1 tsp (5 mL) ground cumin

---

1. Place cucumbers in cold water with ice cubes in a large bowl and let soak for 4 to 8 hours. (This will keep them crunchy until after fermentation.)

2. Prepare brine by dissolving salt and sugar in water.

3. Pack cucumbers into jars (either whole or sliced, as you prefer).

4. Divide grape leaves (if using), garlic, dill, peppercorns, caraway seeds and cumin between the jars. Cover with brine.

5. Close jars and set airlocks. Alternatively, screw lids on jars tightly, but let pressure escape once a day for the first 3 days by unscrewing the rings slightly for a few seconds, then resealing airtight.

6. Let ferment at 64°F to 77°F (18°C to 25°C) for 3 days for "new cucumbers," 7 days for "half sours" or 3 weeks for classic pickles.

To be eaten casually with your hands (never with a fork) before a meal.

Store in the refrigerator for up to 6 months or, to preserve cucumbers for 2 years at room temperature, make preserves by boiling the filled jars for 15 minutes in a boiling water canner. (You can do this with many jarred foods, though it will upset millions of bacteria. With pickles, it's allowed because tradition dictates it.)

"It's the ideal snack."

"I just can't stop myself."

"I eat them in secret at night."

If you have a penchant for pickles, you're not alone. Light and crunchy, they're perfect before a meal, after a marathon or when you have a hangover! Pickles are one of the most common fermented foods. (Of course you're aware that hot dog relish is just jazzed-up diced pickles.) So prepare a few jars for your friends and find out who is a pickle fiend. Once you've unmasked the culprit, you'll always find a willing helper in the kitchen when it's time to make the next batch. A jar or two of your finest should suffice as a reward.

"A meal without kimchi is not a meal," says a Korean proverb. In Korea, it is rare to find a home where people don't ferment their own kimchi, and family recipes are handed down from one generation to the next with great pride. There are as many variations on kimchi as there are homes in Korea. This version from our humble Montreal abodes has managed to win many hearts.

CLASSIC Kimchi

(SPICY KOREAN SAUERKRAUT)

LEVEL OF DIFFICULTY

TYPE OF FERMENTATION
Lactic

PREPARATION TIME
30 minutes

FERMENTATION TIME
3 to 5 days

EQUIPMENT
Scale, fermentation jug or 2-gallon (8 L) pot, small plate (weight), large bowl, 2-quart (2 L) glass jar, airlock (optional)

2% BRINE

6 tbsp + 2 tsp (100 g) sea salt

16 cups (4 L) water, at room temperature

2 lbs 3 oz (1 kg) Chinese cabbage (napa cabbage or giant bok choy)

7 oz (200 g) daikon radish or 1¾ oz (50 g) red radishes (about 5)

7 oz (200 g) carrot (1 large)

7 oz (200 g) yellow onion (1 medium), thinly sliced

2 cloves garlic, minced

2 tsp (10 mL) chopped gingerroot

¼ cup (75 g) gochujang (Korean fermented chili paste) or 1 tbsp (15 mL) Korean hot chile peppers or other ground chile peppers

2 tbsp (30 g) sea salt (or the equivalent to 2% of total weight)

1 tbsp (15 mL) fish sauce or dried shrimp sauce (optional; see tip)

1. In a fermentation jug or large pot, prepare brine by dissolving salt in water. Submerge cabbage, daikon radish and whole carrot. Place a small plate on top as a weight.

2. Let stand overnight (8 to 12 hours).

3. Drain, discarding brine, and rinse cabbage, daikon radish and carrot. Slice cabbage into wide strips ¾ to 1¼ inches (2 to 3 cm) long. Slice daikon and carrot into rounds or strips of ¾ to 1¼ inches (2 to 3 cm) long. Place in a large bowl.

4. Add onion, garlic, ginger, gochujang, salt and fish sauce (if using) to vegetables in bowl. Mix together.

5. Press vegetables into the jar. Use the jar burping technique (see page 38) or an airlock.

6. Let ferment for at least 3 days before tasting (kimchi is usually best after 3 to 4 days of fermentation). If mixture is ready, refrigerate in an airtight container. If not, continue to ferment, tasting every 2 days.

To be eaten in an authentic Bibimbap (page 173), on homemade Pizza (page 180) or on toast with peanut butter...yes, you read that right!

Keeps for 1 year in the refrigerator.

TIP

Fish sauce or dried shrimp sauce will give your kimchi a more pronounced flavor. Kimchi purists will be able to tell that you've added this extra kick to the recipe, but we believe that kimchi is just as tasty without the added sauce.

LEVEL OF DIFFICULTY

TYPE OF FERMENTATION
Lactic

PREPARATION TIME
15 minutes

FERMENTATION TIME
4 to 12 days

EQUIPMENT
Scale, 1-gallon (4 L) wide-mouth jar (a little deeper than the shucked and trimmed ears of corn), weight, airlock (optional)

LACTOFERMENTED *corn* on the *cob*

2% BRINE

4 tbsp (60 g) salt

12 cups (3 L) water, at room temperature

6 to 8 ears of corn, shucked and trimmed

10 tbsp (150 mL) sauerkraut juice or other source of lactobacteria (optional)

1. Prepare brine by dissolving salt in water.

2. Insert ears of corn vertically into the jar. If there is not enough space, cut the ears in two and play Tetris.

3. Add 2% brine until the corn is submerged by at least ½ inch (1 cm) before adding sauerkraut juice or other source of lactobacteria. (This addition is not absolutely necessary, but it will help speed up the fermentation process. Without it, wild bacteria will need to do the job all by themselves.)

4. Place a weight on top of the corn to keep it submerged.

5. Use the jar burping technique (see page 38) or an airlock.

6. Let ferment at room temperature for 4 to 12 days, depending on the temperature and your taste. We recommend you taste it every day after the first 4 days to discover all the subtleties that time adds to the corn's acidity.

To be eaten on the cob, ideally at the end of August while sitting on the steps of the front porch at the cottage. Seb likes it as is. David prefers it boiled and brushed with coconut oil.

Keeps for up to 6 months in a jar in the refrigerator, just to impress visitors.

In the category of easy lactofermentations, corn on the cob is pretty much foolproof. What's more, it's the type of lactofermentation that you can taste each day during the process in order to familiarize yourself with its evolving flavors.

TYPE OF FERMENTATION
Lactic

PREPARATION TIME
30 minutes

FERMENTATION TIME
3 to 4 weeks

EQUIPMENT
Scale, saucepan, bowl, 1-pint (500 mL) glass jar or fermentation jug, pounder (optional), weight, airlock (optional)

18 oz (500 g) fiddleheads

½ cup (50 g) shredded cabbage

1 clove garlic, minced

2 tsp (10 g) sea salt

3 tbsp (45 mL) sauerkraut juice (optional; see page 41)

1 whole cabbage leaf or grape leaf (optional)

2% BRINE (IF NEEDED)

4 tsp (20 g) salt

4 cups (1 L) water, at room temperature

LACTOFERMENTED
Fiddleheads

1. In a saucepan of boiling water, boil fiddleheads for 15 minutes. Rinse thoroughly in cold water to remove the toxins in the raw vegetables. Drain.

2. In a medium bowl, mix together fiddleheads, cabbage, garlic, salt and sauerkraut juice (if using).

3. Transfer to the jar or fermentation jug in small quantities, pressing down vegetables each time by hand or using a pounder.

4. If the liquid produced by the vegetables is insufficient to cover them, prepare 2% brine by dissolving salt in water, then pour enough into jar to cover vegetables.

5. Cover with a cabbage leaf, grape leaf or plastic food wrap and place a weight on top.

6. Use the jar burping technique (see page 38) or an airlock.

7. Let ferment out of direct light for 3 to 4 weeks.

Store these secretly in the door of the fridge and save them for a special occasion. When the time comes, serve them on a salad or use them instead of capers in any kind of dish. In the mood for something exotic? Incorporate the fiddleheads into Misozuke Rolls (page 170).

Keeps for at least 1 year in the refrigerator.

This recipe is no different from other vegetable lactofermentations in a jar, but it is so tasty that we couldn't bear to leave it out of this book or just mention it as an option. If your local grocery store shuns fiddleheads because of their short harvest season, and you want to pick your own baby fiddleheads in the damp woods, make sure you can identify the edible species, as some are toxic.

if they don't grow where you live

TYPE OF FERMENTATION
Lactic

PREPARATION TIME
15 minutes

FERMENTATION TIME
2 to 3 weeks

EQUIPMENT
Scale, bowl, 1-quart (1 L) glass jar, weight, airlock (optional)

lactofermented GRAPE LEAVES

10 ½ oz (300 g) grape leaves (about 50 leaves the size of your hand)

Cold water

4% BRINE
8 tsp (40 g) salt

4 cups (1 L) water, at room temperature

2 cloves garlic

½ bunch fresh dill

1. Wash grape leaves and let soak in a bowl of cold water for 1 hour.

2. Prepare brine by dissolving salt in water.

3. Drain grape leaves. Stack leaves in piles of 6, roll up each pile and pack rolled leaves into the jar. Add garlic and dill.

4. Cover leaves with brine and place a weight on top.

5. Close jar and set airlock. Alternatively, screw lid on jar tightly, but let pressure escape once a day for the first 3 days by unscrewing the ring slightly for a few seconds, then resealing airtight.

6. Let ferment for 2 to 3 weeks. Leaves are ready when their color turns a little darker.

Ideally, use grape leaves that were picked from a garden or plucked surreptitiously from the back lane of your neighbor... who isn't using them anyway.

To be eaten in a roll with sorghum and honey (see page 162), reclining in the nude with a glass of wine in your hand. If the idea makes you uncomfortable, chop the grape leaves into a salad and eat them while wearing your bathing suit.

Keeps for 1 year in the refrigerator.

This elegant fermentation is a lot easier to prepare than the exotic image we have of it. The secret: pick the leaves in the spring while they are still young and tender but are sufficiently large to be rolled up. Once the leaves get too tough, even years of soaking won't make them tasty.

TYPE OF FERMENTATION
Lactic

PREPARATION TIME
Really long, but it's worth the wait

FERMENTATION TIME
12 to 16 weeks

EQUIPMENT
Scale, 5-gallon (20 L) plastic bucket with lid, plate (for a weight), strainer, twelve 1-quart (1 L) jars

Old-Fashioned OLIVES

28 lbs 10 oz (13 kg) fresh green olives (1 standard case)

A lot of water: 2½ gallons (10 L) per day

7 oz (200 g) food-grade sodium hydroxide (optional; see tip)

3¾ cups (900 g) sea salt

Black peppercorns, garlic cloves, cumin or your choice of spice or herb (optional)

Boiling water

1. Rinse olives in plenty of water. Using a paring knife, cut three small notches in each olive (see tip).

2. Place olives in the bucket, cover with water and place a plate on top as a weight to keep them submerged. Keep at room temperature.

3. Rinse olives and change the water every day for 20 days. This step is absolutely essential to remove their bitterness. After every change of water, put plate back in place to keep olives submerged.

4. On Day 20, repeat the procedure, but first be sure to dissolve salt in 40 cups (10 L) water to obtain 9% brine before pouring it over the olives. Put plate back in place and cover with lid to seal bucket airtight.

5. Let ferment for at least 12 weeks before tasting olives. If they are still bitter, let ferment for 4 more weeks.

6. Drain brine and divide olives into jars. Add spices and herbs if desired (although we are of the opinion that nothing holds a candle to the pure and unadorned olive).

7. Fill jars with boiling water and seal airtight while they are still hot, to preserve olives for several years.

TIP

If you find notching the olives too demanding and you can get your hands on some food-grade sodium hydroxide, add 7 oz (200 g) to the water in step 2 and let soak for 3 days. Then, on Day 4, rinse the olives in plenty of water and go directly to step 4. Sodium hydroxide is great if you're lazy, and it will also yield better results. Be careful, because sodium hydroxide is caustic! It needs to be handled with caution, as you would liquid bleach, so wear goggles and gloves and keep it away from young children and animals. That said, sodium hydroxide (also known as lye or caustic soda) is the basic ingredient in all soap. It will not leave a toxic residue on thoroughly rinsed olives. After rinsing the olives four or five times, feel the texture of the water with your fingers. If it is slippery like soap, wash your hands and continue rinsing the olives.

Here, motivation is the main ingredient. Not because the recipe is all that complicated, but because the season for fresh olives is short: just 3 weeks in September. That's your window of opportunity — otherwise, you'll have to wait for the following year.

LEVEL OF DIFFICULTY

TYPE OF FERMENTATION
Lactic

PREPARATION TIME
15 minutes

FERMENTATION TIME
30 days

EQUIPMENT
Scale, bowl, two 1-pint (500 mL) glass jars, weight (optional)

1 lb 5 oz (600 g) lemons or other citrus fruit (about 8 lemons)

5 tsp (25 g) salt

4 whole cloves

2 star anise pods

2 bay leaves

1 cinnamon stick, broken in half

6 tbsp + 2 tsp (100 mL) water

Lemon CONFIT
(PRESERVED LEMONS)

1. Rinse lemons thoroughly in cold water (perhaps a little longer if they are not organic). Cut off tips of lemons and cut lemons into wedges.

2. In a bowl, mix salt with lemon wedges and squash thoroughly with your hands.

3. Press salted lemons into the jars and add cloves, star anise, bay leaves and cinnamon between wedges.

4. Pour water into the bowl to rinse and capture the salt, then pour into jars to cover lemons. Place a weight on top, if necessary to keep lemons submerged. Seal jars airtight.

5. Let ferment out of direct light at room temperature for 30 days.

To be transformed into luscious Lemon Confit Cream (page 183), added to a tajine or eaten as is, with a grimace.

Keeps for 2 years in the refrigerator.

The Lemon Is a Vegetable?

No, lemons are not vegetables (any more than olives or chile peppers are, for that matter), but since the preparation of this recipe follows the logic of vegetable lactofermentations, we declare the lemon an "honorary vegetable" for the duration of this page. Lemon confit with salt may seem bizarre to the uninitiated palate. Nevertheless it is miraculous in desserts and simmered dishes, where the lemons diffuse incredible and unusual flavors. They can also be eaten as is, but not everyone is unanimous on this point.

TYPE OF FERMENTATION
Lactic

PREPARATION TIME
15 minutes

FERMENTATION TIME
90 days

EQUIPMENT
Scale, 1-gallon (4 L) bucket with lid, plate slightly smaller than bucket, weight, airlock, electric dehydrator (optional)

2 lbs 3 oz (1 kg) plums (or cherries or apricots), not too ripe and with no imperfections

2 tbsp (30 mL) vodka or other spirits

6 tbsp + 2 tsp (100 g) salt

¼ cup (60 mL) freshly squeezed lemon juice

Umeboshi Plums
AND UMEBOSHI VINEGAR

1. Wash plums by soaking them in cold water for 1 hour.

2. Trim stems from plums and place fruit in the bucket with vodka. Mix gently with a spoon to sanitize fruit.

3. Discard vodka (in the sink or in your mouth).

4. Add salt and lemon juice to plums, then mix thoroughly.

5. Place a plate on top of plums to cover them completely and add a weight on top. Place lid on bucket, set airlock and ferment for 90 days.

6. Remove lid. The plums should be bathing in a liquid: this is umeboshi vinegar. Strain plums and set vinegar aside.

7. Place plums on racks to dehydrate. Traditionally, we use the summer sun and wait 4 days. If there is no sun (or summer!), place plums in an electric dehydrator for 2 to 3 days or until surface of fruit is slightly whitened by salt deposits.

8. Return plums to umeboshi vinegar and store in the refrigerator.

These can be eaten immediately, but their flavor improves over time. Add to vinaigrettes and marinades, or serve as an accompaniment to brown rice.

Keeps for 2 years in the refrigerator.

After lemons (see previous recipe), it's time for plums to pass for vegetables and flirt with salt. Umeboshi is a Japanese fermentation of ume (pronounced "oo-may"), little sour plums fermented in a large quantity of salt for a few weeks, then partially dried. Acidic, salty and very special, umeboshi is a highly prized seasoning in Japan. Ume plums are difficult to find outside Japan, which is why our recipe uses lemon juice to compensate for the acidity our Western plums lack.

LEVEL OF DIFFICULTY

TYPE OF FERMENTATION
Lactic

PREPARATION TIME
30 minutes

FERMENTATION TIME
45 days

EQUIPMENT
Scale, 1-quart (1 L) glass jar,
weight, airlock (optional)

Muscovite GARLIC SCAPES

4% BRINE
8 tsp (40 g) salt
4 cups (1 L) water, at room temperature

18 oz (500 g) garlic scapes
1 whole cabbage leaf (optional)

1. Prepare brine by dissolving salt in water.
2. Remove and discard heads of garlic scapes. Cut stalks into pieces 2 to 6 inches (5 to 15 cm) long.
3. Press stalks into the jar without crushing them. Cover with brine. Cover surface with cabbage leaf or plastic food wrap. Set a weight on top.
4. Close jar and set airlock. Alternatively, screw lid on jar tightly, but let pressure escape once a day for the first 3 days by unscrewing the ring slightly for a few seconds, then resealing airtight.
5. Let ferment for 45 days.

Fermented garlic scapes are a delight when ground and added discreetly to a vinaigrette or spicy sauce. Try them in a sun-dried tomato tapenade (page 157), garnished with sourdough croutons for the next vampire hunt.

Keeps for more than 1 year in the refrigerator.

LEVEL OF DIFFICULTY

TYPES OF TRANSFORMATION
Caramelization, lactic fermentation

PREPARATION TIME
5 minutes

TRANSFORMATION TIME
20 to 25 days

FERMENTATION TIME
According to your level of patience

EQUIPMENT
Rice cooker

BLACK Garlic

10 heads garlic

1. Place whole garlic heads in a rice cooker, cover, set cooker to Reheat mode and leave on for 20 to 25 days. The garlic cloves will undergo a chemical transformation that will turn them completely black and give them a delightful buttery texture.

2. Store at room temperature, in an airtight container, to allow the flavors to further develop.

Spread on sourdough bread and garnish with slices of avocado and seaweed (see page 158), or add to sauces and vinaigrettes to delight your guests. Or just eat them like jujubes...well, maybe not, but they're that good!

Keeps for 1 year at room temperature in an airtight container.

Here we reveal a well-kept secret in the kitchens of great chefs: black garlic. During the 3-week transformation period, the strong flavor and pungent character of the garlic gives way to flavors of sweet and smoked nuts, which will add unique, rich caramelized notes to a variety of dishes. Most of the process of transformation here is caramelization. Once the transformation is complete, the lactic fermentation process springs to life and helps develop the richness of the flavors. Black garlic is a rare commodity, and when one manages to find some, it costs a fortune. However, it is very inexpensive to make and not very complicated. So there — now you have a business opportunity! As for us, we are already pretty busy.

LEVEL OF DIFFICULTY

TYPE OF FERMENTATION
Lactic

PREPARATION TIME
30 minutes

FERMENTATION TIME
48 hours

RESTING TIME
10 days

EQUIPMENT
Scale, two 1-cup (250 mL) glass jars, 4- to 8-cup (1 to 2 L) saucepan, fine-mesh sieve, bowl, blender or food processor, whisk

---

$^3/_4$ cup (90 g) yellow mustard powder or seeds

2 tsp (10 g) salt

$^1/_4$ cup (60 mL) water

7 oz (200 g) white onion (1 medium), finely chopped

3 cloves garlic, minced

$^1/_2$ cup (125 mL) white wine or fruit wine

$^1/_2$ cup (125 mL) fruit vinegar or Apple Cider Vinegar (page 99)

$^7/_8$ oz (25 g) fresh turmeric, peeled and sliced, or $^1/_2$ tsp (2 mL) ground turmeric (for color)

Mustard

1. In a jar, mix mustard and salt in water. Seal jar and let ferment at 68°F to 86°F (20°C to 30°C) for 48 hours.

2. In a saucepan, over low heat, simmer onion, garlic, wine and vinegar for 15 minutes to bring out flavors.

3. Using a sieve, strain onion mixture into a bowl to save liquid. Save solid pieces for your next sautéed dish.

4. In a blender or food processor, purée wine mixture and turmeric with fermented mustard mixture.

5. Transfer to a clean saucepan. Bring to a boil over low heat, whisking to prevent burning. As soon as mixture starts to boil, remove from heat.

6. Transfer mixture, while still hot, into clean glass jars and seal.

7. Let stand at room temperature for 10 days. The mustard will lose some of its pungency and achieve a more delicate flavor during this little rest period.

Use without skimping on anything that goes nicely with the color yellow.

Keeps in the refrigerator forever and then some!

LEVEL OF DIFFICULTY

TYPE OF FERMENTATION
Lactic

PREPARATION TIME
15 minutes

FERMENTATION TIME
2 to 5 days

EQUIPMENT
Bowl, 1-pint (500 mL) glass jar

CHUNKY chutney

3 small mangos, diced
2 cloves garlic, minced
1 dried hot chile pepper, minced, or 2 tbsp (30 mL) hot pepper flakes
½ cup (65 g) toasted unsweetened coconut flakes
1 tsp (5 mL) grated gingerroot
1 tsp (5 mL) cumin seeds
½ tsp (2 g) sea salt
½ cup (125 mL) water
¼ cup (60 mL) sauerkraut juice (optional; see tip)
2 tbsp (30 mL) freshly squeezed lime juice
2 stalks lemongrass, cut to fit jar

1. In a bowl, using your hands, mix mangos, garlic, chile pepper, coconut, ginger, cumin seeds, salt, water, sauerkraut juice (if using) and lime juice.

2. Transfer mixture to the jar and add lemongrass.

3. Seal jar and let ferment naturally at room temperature for 2 days if using sauerkraut juice; otherwise, wait up to 5 days. In case of an insatiable craving for chutney, forget the rules and open the jar on the second day.

To be eaten with labneh on hot naan (page 121). It will also transform just about any bland food or disappointing recipe into an original and memorable dish.

Keeps for 2 months in the refrigerator.

TIP

Adding sauerkraut juice helps accelerate the fermentation process and brings you closer to the day when you'll be able to enjoy the chutney. You can also leave fermentation to chance by leaving the chutney on the table for a few days. All depends on your preference and your sense of adventure.

We have long debated the importance of fermentation in this recipe, because chutney can also be eaten fresh. But because it gets better with time, why not make it a lactofermentation and enjoy the fruits of probiotics? One essential thing we both agree on: this chutney is really good.

LEVEL OF DIFFICULTY

TYPES OF FERMENTATION
Lactic, acetic

PREPARATION TIME
15 minutes

FERMENTATION TIME
45 days

EQUIPMENT
Scale, gloves, blender, two
1-cup (250 mL) glass jars,
airlocks (optional)

BAJAN
Hot Pepper
SAUCE

7 oz (200 g) Scotch bonnet
or habanero chile peppers
(the choice of peppers
will determine the flavor
and strength of the sauce;
sweet peppers can be
substituted in part or
in whole)

3½ oz (100 g) yellow
onion (½ onion), coarsely
chopped

1¾ oz (50 g) fresh turmeric,
peeled and sliced, or 2 tsp
(10 mL) ground turmeric

2 tsp (10 mL) mustard seeds

1 tsp (5 mL) cane sugar

4 tsp (20 g) salt

1¼ cups (300 mL) water

1 tsp (5 mL) apple cider
vinegar, kombucha vinegar
or white vinegar (optional)

4% BRINE (IF NEEDED)

2 tsp (10 g) salt

1 cup (250 mL) water, at
room temperature

1. Put on gloves and scoop seeds out of peppers (or don't, if you want an ultra-hot sauce that will warm you instantly over the long winter).

2. In a blender, purée chile peppers, onion, turmeric, mustard seeds, sugar, salt and water until mixture is uniform and pourable. Add a little 4% brine if necessary, to thin it. The mustard grains will absorb the water, so it's normal if the mixture seems too liquid.

3. Transfer mixture to the jars. Close and set airlocks (if using). Alternatively, screw lids on jars tightly, but let pressure escape once a day for the first 3 days by unscrewing the rings slightly for a few seconds, then resealing airtight.

4. Let ferment at room temperature for 45 days.

5. Open and taste. If it is too hot, add vinegar to balance the flavor.

Use on any food that's short on personality and, while eating it, try your best to hide the fact that you've added a bit too much.

Keeps for 1 year in the refrigerator.

TYPES OF FERMENTATION
Lactic, alcoholic

PREPARATION TIME
15 minutes

FERMENTATION TIME
3 to 7 days

EQUIPMENT
Scale, pressure juicer or centrifugal juicer (or blender/ food processor, fine-mesh sieve, cheesecloth and bowl), 1-quart (1 L) glass jar, airlock (optional)

2 lbs 3 oz (1 kg) carrots or other root vegetables, such as beets

¼ yellow onion

3½ oz (100 g) cabbage

1 packet (5 g) lactic acid starter culture or 2 tbsp (30 mL) sauerkraut juice

2 tsp (10 g) salt (or 1% of total weight of vegetable juice)

Kvass is a fermented vegetable juice that is very popular in Russia. Its flavor is rather difficult to describe: somewhere between V8 and kombucha.

VEGETABLE Kvass

1. Peel carrots. This step is optional, but it will improve the flavor of the juice.

2. Run carrots, onion and cabbage through a juicer. Alternatively, place vegetables in a blender, cover and blend until liquefied. Pour into a fine-mesh sieve lined with cheesecloth and let juice drain into a bowl.

3. Pour juice into the jar and add starter culture. Add salt in a ratio of 1% of the weight of the juice and mix well.

4. Close jar and set airlock. Alternatively, screw lid on jar tightly, but let pressure escape once a day for the first 3 days by unscrewing the ring slightly for a few seconds, then resealing airtight.

5. Let ferment for 3 to 7 days, to your taste.

To drink when the rooster crows, even before brushing your teeth. It is also a worthy substitute for tomato juice in a Bloody Mary.

Keeps for 2 months in the refrigerator in the same jar or in hermetically sealed bottles.

TIP

Advice for those of you who are in a hurry: buy raw cold-pressed juice from the store and start at step 3!

Fruit,
sugar and honey

Because everyone loves bubbles

WHEN WE THINK ABOUT FERMENTED FRUIT AND SUGAR, we think of vinegar, sweet alcohol, bubbles and evenings to remember. The world of sweet fermentations is a little more temperamental than that of vegetables, and a lot more sensitive to time, temperature and ambient contaminants. In just a few days, your precious nectar may turn to vinegar; overnight, your vat could be visited by fruit flies; and in just seconds, your kombucha culture may frighten off a guest who wasn't quite ready to meet your "mom." In this chapter, we introduce you to some recipes that are surprisingly simple. Once you've mastered these, you'll look forward to concocting other delightful potions.

IN SEARCH OF A MOTHER...

Although a few recipes can be started spontaneously with ambient yeasts, most sugar fermentations require that you start with a specific culture. A kombucha mother, kefir grains, champagne or bread yeasts, and apple cider vinegar with a mother can all be found close to home or online, but you may need to search a little (see Where to Buy This Strange Stuff, page 197, for pointers). Once you have your culture, a single strain of it will last a lifetime, provided you maintain it. The truth is, everyone forgets to take care of their ferments at one time or another, leaving them to languish or die at the back of the fridge. That's why we're happy to share our healthy ferments with the people around us. It's a guarantee that we will always find someone in our circle with a hale and hearty specimen to donate.

DO I WASH OR SANITIZE?

For mixed fermentations like water kefir and kombucha, washing your containers and tools with dish soap and hot water is sufficient. For more sensitive fermentations made from pure yeast cultures, such as cider, mead and beer, you will need to sanitize as well as wash to prevent contamination. Always rinse with clear water to remove any residue (see details on page 23).

WHAT DO I NEED TO KNOW ABOUT THE ENVIRONMENT?

As a general rule for sugar, the warmer the environment, the faster the fermentation. However, as the hare and the tortoise have taught us, speed is not always a good thing. Lower and more stable temperatures are more likely to yield products of higher quality. Darkness (or at least the absence of direct sunlight) is also an advantage. The final determining factor is the amount of oxygen in the environment. Alcoholic fermentations must avoid contact with oxygen as much as possible. Filling bottles and carboys to full capacity and hermetically sealing them helps minimize the amount of air to which fermentations are exposed. For the same reason, airlocks need to be sealed and their water levels adequately maintained. The opposite is true for water kefir, kombucha and acetic fermentations in general. These fermentations require an aerated environment and are typically created in open jars with breathable fabric stretched over the mouth to keep out insects.

SO WHERE ARE THE BUBBLES?

Transforming a fermented liquid into a carbonated beverage requires a second fermentation — this time in an anaerobic (oxygen-free) environment, in a bottle at room temperature. Some of the sugar in the liquid is turned into carbon dioxide, but since the bottle is sealed, it accumulates in the beer or kombucha and is released as bubbles once the bottle is opened. Beer and mead need to have sugar added at the time of bottling. This is because their fermentations are complete; that is, all of the fermentable sugar has already been transformed by the time the liquid is being bottled. Adding sugar at this stage continues the fermentation process to produce the desired effervescence. Kombucha and water kefir, on the other hand, are fermentations that still contain sugar at the time of bottling, so it is not necessary to add more. Remember, there is always a risk of bottles breaking if the contents ferment too much. Use sturdy bottles, open them carefully and follow the recommended fermentation time guidelines.

IS THIS WHITE/BROWN/GELATINOUS STUFF NORMAL OR DANGEROUS?

Always rely on your nose, eyes and instinct. As a general rule, these fermentations are safe, because the alcohol in them prevents the proliferation of bad bacteria. The low pH of water kefir and kombucha make them very acidic, which also helps protect them from bad bacteria. If white, gray or blue mold appears on kombucha, it's better to throw away the culture and start over. If there are white, gelatinous clusters on the surface, this indicates new cultures, which means your fermentation is working like a charm! Don't worry if you see dark clouds mixed up in the mother. This is not mold, but the residue of tea and clumps of cultures.

FERMENTED HONEY WITH GARLIC (PAGE 79)

This garlic—flavored honey is the secret ingredient that will take your vinaigrettes to a new level. Add variety by infusing the honey with lavender flowers, calendula, hemp or other dried herbs (before, after or during fermentation).

TYPES OF FERMENTATION
Lactic, alcoholic

PREPARATION TIME
2 minutes + 30 seconds per day

FERMENTATION TIME
1 month

EQUIPMENT
1-cup (250 mL) glass jar, weight

1 cup (150 g) garlic cloves

¾ cup (180 mL) unpasteurized honey

FERMENTED Honey WITH Garlic

1. Peel garlic cloves. Discard any cloves that are damaged or brown. Place garlic cloves in a glass jar and cover with honey. Use a weight to keep garlic cloves submerged. Seal airtight.

2. Let ferment at room temperature. For the first 2 weeks, gently shake jar every day to thoroughly mix honey with the liquid being released from the garlic and to submerge stray garlic cloves. During the first week, every 2 days, release the gases that have accumulated by slightly unscrewing the ring of the jar for a few seconds, then sealing airtight.

3. Let stand for another 2 weeks. By then, the honey will have turned much more liquid, almost like water.

To use in absolutely all of your vinaigrettes, as an atomic flu buster or in the eyes of your worst enemy. The garlic can be removed and used the same way you would use fresh garlic cloves.

The mixture keeps for years at room temperature.

LEVEL OF DIFFICULTY

TYPES OF FERMENTATION
Acetic; alcoholic (3%) for beverage

PREPARATION TIME
20 minutes for shrub syrup and 1 minute for beverage

FERMENTATION TIME
1 month for shrub syrup and 2 to 4 days for beverage

EQUIPMENT
Shrub syrup: Scale, 4-cup (1 L) saucepan, 1-quart (1 L) glass jar with airtight lid

Beverage: 1-quart (1 L) bottle or glass jar with airtight lid

SHRUB SYRUP

3¾ cups (750 g) cane sugar

1 cup (250 mL) Apple Cider Vinegar (page 99) or Kombucha Vinegar (page 89)

2 lb 3 oz (1 kg) field berries (blueberries or other small fruits from your harvest)

SHRUB SPARKLING BEVERAGE

½ cup (125 mL) shrub syrup

3 cups (750 mL) water

A few grains bread yeast or champagne yeast

Shrub SYRUP AND sparkling beverage

SHRUB SYRUP

1. In a saucepan, over low heat, dissolve sugar in vinegar, stirring constantly. Let cool to room temperature.

2. Thoroughly rinse berries and transfer to the jar.

3. Pour room-temperature vinegar over berries. Seal airtight and gently shake to thoroughly cover fruit.

4. Let ferment at room temperature for 1 month before consuming. Strain out the berries, or don't.

Refreshment guaranteed: 2 tbsp (30 mL) of this syrup in 1 cup (250 mL) sparkling water — with or without gin. And if you have a cocktail recipe that didn't mix up to your liking, add some shrub syrup!

Keeps in your bar at room temperature for 1 year.

SHRUB SPARKLING BEVERAGE

1. In a bottle or jar, mix shrub syrup with water. Add yeast grains.

2. Close bottle and let ferment at room temperature for 2 to 4 days. Open bottle to check effervescence.

3. When ready, keep beverage in refrigerator to prevent it from exploding.

To enjoy with ice cubes and a beatific smile on your lips: you've just saved the day's salary it would have cost you to purchase a carbonated water machine.

Keeps for 30 days in the refrigerator.

Shrubs are fermented syrups that can be made with any fruit that is available. They make fabulous aromatic syrups for cocktails and coulis to pour over desserts.

Here is one of the book's signature recipes that is guaranteed to impress! (We give you the right to usurp our intellectual property and say you thought of it yourself.)

There are two versions of this recipe: one with added yeast and the other using wild yeast already present on the fruit. Both recipes yield good results, but adding yeast speeds up the process and placates the impatient.

In case of spills, use boiling water to remove the beeswax. To avoid this unpleasant task and the animated discussion that will ensue with your roommate or significant other, it's best to cover your work surfaces with newspaper.

Vinified Fruits
IN BEESWAX

LEVEL OF DIFFICULTY

TYPE OF FERMENTATION
Alcoholic

PREPARATION TIME
1 to 2 hours

FERMENTATION TIME
2 days to 3 weeks, depending on whether yeast is added

EQUIPMENT
Scale, small bowl and toothpicks (if using yeast), small deep saucepan, foil, clothespins, safety pins, thick cord or cheesecloth to hang fruit, pillowcase (if necessary)

Champagne or bread yeast (optional)

3 tbsp + 1 tsp (50 mL) warm water (if using yeast)

10 to 15 ripe fruits with stem, depending on size (plums, apricots, figs, kiwis, cherries or other soft fruits with a skin)

18 oz (500 g) beeswax

1. Optional: If using yeast, mix it with warm water in a small bowl. To start the yeast, dip a toothpick in yeast mixture, then insert toothpick a few millimeters into the fruit. Repeat procedure two or three times in different places on each fruit.

2. Line interior of small saucepan with foil. Place wax in foil in saucepan and melt over low heat just until fluid, without heating it too much. (Smoking wax can kill the yeasts on the skin of the fruit.)

3. Working with one piece of fruit at a time, place a clothespin on the stem. Holding fruit by the clothespin, dip fruit in beeswax. Let set for a few seconds, then dip again, five to seven times, until fruit is completely coated in wax. Remove clothespin and fasten safety pin to stem. Pin fruit to a cord or hanging cheesecloth. Repeat with the remaining fruits.

4. In winter, the fruits can ferment as is, in the air, without much risk of a fruit fly invasion. In summer, all fruits need to be protected by a pillowcase or another type of shelter to keep insects away.

5. The fruits will ferment inside the wax. Deprived of oxygen, they will not grow mold and will turn effervescent. Once the wax cracks or juice brims over the base of the stem — after 2 or 3 days for fruits with yeast added or 2 to 3 weeks for fruits without added yeast — the fruits are ready to eat. Not all the fruits will be ready at the same time. You can look forward to a daily harvest!

Cut in half and served with chocolate shavings, vinified fruits can be eaten like oysters! An exotic treat for a romantic evening for two or to share with your adventurous friends.

If you want to eat all the fruit at the same time (for example, on a special occasion), store the fermented fruits in their wax shells in the fridge for a few days, until all of them are ready.

TIP

If your fruit doesn't have a strong stem, wrap a string around the fruit to hold it and to pin it up. Dental floss seems to do the trick.

LEVEL OF DIFFICULTY

WATER Kefir

TYPES OF FERMENTATION
Lactic, acetic, slightly alcoholic (~0.5%)

PREPARATION TIME
20 minutes

FERMENTATION TIME
36 to 72 hours

EQUIPMENT
1-gallon (4 L) glass jar, cheesecloth (optional), breathable fabric, elastic band or string, fine-mesh sieve, airtight bottles, airtight glass container

FOR 16 CUPS (4 L)

14 cups (3.5 L) water, at room temperature

1 cup + 1½ tbsp (180 g) cane sugar

¼ cup (44 g) or more (as much as you have) water kefir grains or a packet of kefir powder (see note 1, page 87)

1 citrus fruit of your choice, peeled and sliced

1 handful of raisins (or dried figs, to be more sophisticated)

TO PRESERVE WATER KEFIR GRAINS

1 tbsp (15 mL) granulated, brown or cane sugar

1 cup (250 mL) water, at room temperature

1. Pour water into the jar, add sugar and stir to dissolve. Add kefir grains, citrus slices and dried fruit. If desired, wrap grains (or fruit) in a piece of cheesecloth to prevent a dilemma later when sorting (is that a raisin or a kefir grain?).

2. Cover mouth of jar with fabric that allows air (but not insects) to pass through and attach with an elastic band or string.

3. Let ferment out of direct light at room temperature. Taste mixture at set intervals. Kefir is best between 36 and 72 hours of fermentation. At this time, the dried fruit will rise to the surface, propelled by carbon dioxide bubbles.

4. Filter water kefir through a fine-mesh sieve, straining out kefir grains and fruit. Separate grains from fruit; discard fruit. Preserve grains for future use (see below).

5. Drink water kefir immediately or bottle and refrigerate to prevent explosions.

TO PRESERVE WATER KEFIR GRAINS

1. Prepare sweetened water by stirring sugar into water until dissolved.

2. Transfer kefir grains to a glass container and cover with sweetened water. Seal airtight and refrigerate until you are ready to use the grains again (they will stay alive for up to 3 weeks). Strain off liquid before using grains.

To drink on the beach...or, if you're not quite so fortunate, on a bench next to your neighborhood public swimming pool.

Keeps for 5 days in the refrigerator (the beverage will become increasingly effervescent).

Continued on page 87

Water kefir costs next to nothing to make, requires almost no equipment, can be prepared in a few minutes, ferments in 24 hours, is chock-full of millions of probiotics and has a lower sugar content than any juice on the market. On top of that, it's fizzy. Who could ask for anything more?

WATER Kefir ... CONTINUED

Q&A

1. What is the difference between kefir grains and kefir powder? *Kefir grains are found in their natural state; they contain a wider variety of microorganisms than kefir powder (starter culture) and can be reused indefinitely. If you used kefir powder to make water kefir, you can use ¼ cup (60 mL) water kefir as your starter for a new batch; however, doing so more than three or four times is not recommended, as the culture becomes imbalanced and does not ferment as well. Kefir grains are more economical in the long run, but if you only want to make kefir once or plan to make it only a few times a year, you can choose the powdered form. If you use the grains, pass them along to your neighbor when you're done and get them back when you need them again.*

2. What is the difference between water kefir grains and milk kefir grains? *See Milk Kefir, page 108.*

3. I bought dried grains. How do I start? *Condition dried water kefir grains before use by mixing them with 2 cups (500 mL) water sweetened with ½ cup (125 mL) cane sugar, or according to package directions. Let ferment for 1 week at room temperature in an open glass jar with breathable fabric stretched over the mouth.*

If you are making milk kefir (page 108) and have purchased dried milk kefir grains, condition them with 1 cup (250 mL) water sweetened with 3 tbsp (45 mL) cane sugar, or according to package directions, then let ferment as for water kefir grains.

4. I forgot to feed my grains. I'm afraid they may be too old! *We worry about getting old, too. Condition the grains by following the same method as for dried grains, but let them ferment for only 2 days.*

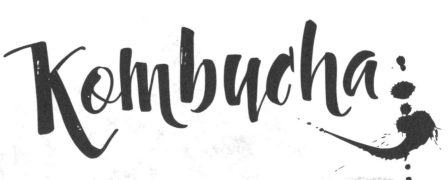

Kombucha

TYPES OF FERMENTATION
Acetic, slightly alcoholic
(~0.5%)

PREPARATION TIME
20 minutes

FERMENTATION TIME
9 to 16 days

EQUIPMENT
Large pot, fine-mesh sieve, bowl, 1-gallon (4 L) glass or food-grade plastic fermentation container with a wide mouth, breathable fabric, elastic band or string, 2-cup (500 mL) airtight container, cotton filter or clean cloth (optional), airtight bottles

FOR 8 CUPS (2 L)

7 cups (1.75 L) water, divided

4 standard bags (12 g total) green, black or white tea (both premium brands and regular commercial brands will do the job, whereas chamomile and other more oily herbs can weaken the culture)

⅔ cup (120 g) granulated, cane or brown sugar

Kombucha culture: kombucha mother + 1 cup (250 mL) kombucha

Aromatics to taste: aromatic herbs, medicinal plants, fruit, concentrated infusion, hydrosols (see suggestions on page 89)

Gingerroot (optional)

1. In a large pot, bring 2 cups (500 mL) water almost to a boil (203F°/95°C). Add tea bags and let steep for 5 minutes. Strain through a fine-mesh sieve placed over a bowl and let cool.

2. Add sugar to tea and stir until dissolved. At this point, the mixture is too highly concentrated and sweet to drink, unless you're a Berber.

3. Pour mixture into fermentation container, add 5 cups (1.25 L) cold water and mix well. Let cool.

4. Add kombucha culture (mother + liquid) to lukewarm sweet tea. The 1-gallon (4 L) container should be half full. Cover mouth of jar with fabric that allows air (but not insects) to pass through and attach with an elastic band or string.

5. Let ferment in a dark area at 73°F to 82°F (23°C to 28°C) for 8 to 14 days. The kombucha will turn less sweet and more acidic.

6. Starting on the 8th day, taste every 2 days. When the sugar/acid balance satisfies your palate, set aside 2 cups (500 mL) liquid along with the mother in an airtight container in the refrigerator for future brewing (this will be enough for about 16 cups /4 L). The mother will stay alive for up to 6 months between each use.

7. Optional: To minimize the amount of sediment in the finished product, line the sieve with a cotton filter or clean cloth and filter kombucha.

8. Flavor kombucha according to taste, in a concentrated infusion or by adding aromatics according to what's in season. Let ferment from a few hours to a few days, as desired.

9. Filter out any solid aromatics and pour kombucha into bottles. Seal well and store in a warm, dark area (77°F to 95°F/25°C to 35°C) to start a second fermentation that will turn the kombucha effervescent. A few slices of ginger, or a little bit of any juice you have on hand, can speed up this second fermentation.

10. Check level of effervescence by opening bottles every day. Once it is to your taste, store bottles in the refrigerator to stop the secondary fermentation and stabilize the bubbles.

You have become a kombucha brewer! Now you can start your own business and multiply your mothers until there is an overabundance.

SUGGESTIONS FOR AROMATICS

- **Mint and Chlorophyll:** *A few leaves fresh mint + 1 tbsp (15 mL) liquid chlorophyll*

- **Rose and Schisandra:** *¼ cup (5 g) edible rose petals + 1 tbsp (15 mL) dried schisandra berries, ground in a coffee mill*

- **Hibiscus and Rose Hip:** *3 tbsp (45 mL) hibiscus flowers + 1 tbsp (15 mL) rose hips*

- **Ginger:** *3 tbsp (45 mL) fresh ginger juice*

- **Garden Harvest:** *1 or 2 handfuls of aromatic herbs: lemon balm leaves (try them!), mint, basil, sage, lemongrass, chamomile flowers, fruit tree blossoms or rose petals*

- **Brewer's Lemonade:** *3 lemons, sliced (you can even use rinsed lemons from Lemon Confit, page 59) + 1 tsp (5 g) sea salt + 1 bunch chopped shiso, basil or lemon balm leaves*

- **The Diva:** *2 cucumbers, sliced + 1 bunch fresh mint, finely chopped*

KOMBUCHA VINEGAR

To make kombucha vinegar, let prepared kombucha ferment at room temperature in a wide-mouth jar covered with breathable fabric for 2 to 6 months before bottling. The kombucha will remain clear and very acidic — perfect for drizzling over salads or for making a shrub (see page 80)! Always keep at room temperature.

Anyone can make an excellent kombucha; it's simple, inexpensive, quick and fun. The flavor is a bit of a surprise at first, but is so pleasant you'll get hooked on it. Kombucha originated in imperial China. This sparkling fermented tea is so popular it's starting to replace the traditional carbonated beverages served in trendy cafés and restaurants. The kombucha mother is a pancake of gelatinous cellulose that has been shared like a "mushroom of friendship" for generations. It is a complex starter culture — a nest of yeasts and bacteria that coexist in harmony. You will need to find a mother soaking in a little kombucha to begin your home brewing.

KOMBUCHA (PAGE 88)

Jun
(HONEY—BASED KOMBUCHA)

TYPES OF FERMENTATION
Acetic, slightly alcoholic
(~0.5%)

PREPARATION TIME
25 minutes

FERMENTATION TIME
About 10 days

EQUIPMENT
Large pot, fine-mesh sieve, bowl, 1-gallon (4 L) glass or food-grade plastic container with a wide mouth, breathable fabric, elastic band or string, 2-cup (500 mL) airtight container, cotton filter or clean cloth, airtight bottles

FOR 16 CUPS (4 L)

13 cups (3.25 L) water, at room temperature, divided

2 standard bags (6 g total) green or black tea

1 cup (250 mL) unpasteurized honey

Aromatics and other infusions to taste (see Suggestions)

Kombucha/jun culture: kombucha mother + 2 cups (500 mL) kombucha or jun

1. In a large pot, bring 4 cups (1 L) water almost to a boil (203F°/95°C). Add tea bags and let steep for 10 minutes. Strain through a fine-mesh sieve placed over a bowl and let cool.

2. Pour honey into the 1-gallon (4 L) container. Add ¾ cup + 2 tbsp (200 mL) room-temperature water and shake until honey is dissolved. Important: never use hot water, as it will destroy the wild yeasts naturally present in the honey.

3. Add the remaining water and cooled tea. Mix well. Add aromatics, if desired.

4. Add kombucha/jun culture (mother + liquid). Cover mouth of jar with fabric that allows air (but not insects) to pass through and attach with an elastic band or string.

5. Let ferment in a dark area at 68°F to 77°F (20°C to 25°C) for about 8 days, tasting regularly.

6. When flavor is satisfactory, set aside mother and 2 cups (500 mL) liquid in an airtight container and store in the refrigerator for the next brewing.

7. Line the sieve with a cotton filter or clean cloth and filter jun before pouring it into airtight bottles.

8. Let ferment in bottles in a dark area at 77°F to 95°F (25°C to 35°C) for a few days, until jun is sufficiently effervescent. Refrigerate.

Keeps for up to 6 months in the refrigerator.

SUGGESTIONS FOR INFUSIONS
Like kombucha, jun can be flavored, but traditionally the aromatics are added at the start of fermentation. Here are a few examples.

Instead of black tea, infuse with:

- *Jasmine: 3 tsp (15 mL) jasmine tea. Maybe the best jun flavor that exists!*
- *Maté: 4 tsp (20 mL) maté. For a jun that wakes you up!*

Add to warm black tea infusion:

- *Raspberry or cherry: 1 cup (170 g) whole fresh raspberries or 1 cup (175 g) crushed cherries. To be consumed in the company of a yoga mat.*
- *Tonic: Grated zest of 2 oranges and 1 cup (100 g) fresh dandelion flowers. To serve as an aperitif, with ice cubes, with or without gin.*

Many fermentation aficionados consider jun (pronounced "djun") an exceptional and sophisticated distant cousin to kombucha. In fact, jun is nothing more than kombucha made with honey instead of cane sugar. The honey gives it a more refined flavor, but also makes it quite a bit more expensive to produce. The recipe for jun is similar to that of kombucha, but the flavor in the end is sweeter and subtler.

Ginger bug is a spontaneous ginger starter traditionally made in the Caribbean. Ginger and sugar feed the wild yeasts that settle in it. In a few days, the yeasts multiply to turn the sweet mixture into an acidic and effervescent liquid. This ferment base is used to make ginger beer. Don't be fooled by the name — ginger beer contains very little alcohol (about 0.5%), so you needn't worry about serving it to the entire family.

LEVEL OF DIFFICULTY

TYPES OF FERMENTATION
Lactic, slightly alcoholic
(~0.5%)

PREPARATION TIME
5 minutes every 2 days

FERMENTATION TIME
7 days

EQUIPMENT
1-quart (1 L) glass jar,
breathable fabric, elastic band
or string

Ginger BUG

STARTER CULTURE FOR 7 DAYS

3 cups (750 mL) water

11 tsp (55 mL) granulated sugar

4 tsp (20 mL) grated gingerroot

TO DIVIDE AS FOLLOWS:

Day 1: 3 tbsp + 1 tsp (50 mL) water + 1 tsp (5 mL) sugar + 1 tsp (5 mL) ginger

Day 3: 6 tbsp + 2 tsp (100 mL) water + 2 tsp (10 mL) sugar + 1 tsp (5 mL) ginger

Day 5: ¾ cup + 2 tbsp (200 mL) water + 4 tsp (20 mL) sugar + 1 tsp (5 mL) ginger

Day 7: 1⅔ cups (400 mL) water + 4 tsp (20 mL) sugar + 1 tsp (5 mL) ginger

1. In the jar, mix ingredients for Day 1. Cover mouth of jar with fabric that allows air (but not insects) to pass through and attach with an elastic band or string.

2. Let ferment in a warm area, between 77°F and 95°F (25°C and 35°C).

3. Gently shake jar a few times a day for 7 days.

4. On days 3, 5 and 7, add ingredients according to the list.

5. When mixture begins to produce bubbles (between 3 and 7 days), it is ready to be used.

6. Continue to feed starter culture every 2 days (each time doubling the amounts of ginger and water, but not the sugar) to keep it active, or else keep it "dormant" in the refrigerator for up to 2 months. All you need is to place it in a warm area and feed it to reawaken it!

Use ginger bug to brew your own ginger beer and root beer (see page 96). You can also use it as a starter culture for bread (see page 118). Simply substitute the quantity of water normally used for a flour starter culture with the same quantity of ginger bug.

TYPES OF FERMENTATION
**Acetic, slightly alcoholic
(lactic 0.5%)**

PREPARATION TIME
30 minutes each

FERMENTATION TIME
**3 to 5 days for ginger beer;
3 to 10 days for root beer**

EQUIPMENT
Ginger beer: **Scale, 1-gallon (4 L)
glass jar, breathable fabric,
elastic band or string, 1-quart
(1 L) glass jar, airtight glass
bottles**

Root beer: **Coffee grinder or
mortar and pestle, large pot,
fine-mesh sieve, bowl, airtight
glass bottles**

ginger BEER AND root BEER

FOR 16 CUPS (4 L) GINGER BEER

1 cup + 3 tbsp (240 g) cane sugar

7 oz (200 g) grated fresh ginger

About 3 cups (750 mL) Ginger Bug (page 95)

12 cups (3 L) water

FOR 16 CUPS (4 L) ROOT BEER

Dried aromatics blend (see opposite page)

16 cups (4 L) water

1 tsp (5 mL) vanilla extract or 1 vanilla bean

1½ cups (375 mL) light (fancy) molasses

Lemon juice (optional)

Cane sugar (optional)

1 cup (250 mL) Ginger Bug (page 95)

GINGER BEER

1. Wash and sanitize equipment (see page 23).

2. In the 1-gallon (4 L) jar, mix sugar, grated ginger, ginger bug and water. Cover mouth of jar with fabric that allows air (but not insects) to pass through and attach with an elastic band or string.

3. Let ferment in a warm area, between 77°F and 95°F (25°C and 35°C), for 1 to 3 days, depending on the temperature. Taste. It's ready once you like it.

4. Set aside some ginger beer in a 1-quart (1 L) glass jar in the refrigerator for your next brewing; this is your ginger bug that you will need to feed (see page 95, step 6).

5. Sanitize bottles, then bottle the rest of the ginger beer airtight. Continue fermentation in bottles for 2 days, always between 77°F and 95°F (25°C and 35°C) to increase effervescence.

6. Refrigerate to prevent bottles from exploding.

To be drunk barefoot while listening to reggae music.

ROOT BEER

1. Coarsely grind dried aromatics in coffee grinder or crush with mortar and pestle into pieces about ⅛ inch (3 mm) in size.

2. In a large pot, bring water to a boil. Add ground aromatics, reduce heat to low, cover and simmer gently for 1 hour to infuse. Add vanilla 10 minutes before the end.

3. Remove from heat, add molasses and stir to dissolve.

4. Strain mixture through a fine-mesh sieve into a bowl, discarding solids. Let cool to 98.5°F (37°C) or less. Taste, then add lemon juice and/or sugar to suit your palate. Stir in ginger bug.

5. Sanitize bottles (see page 23), then bottle the mixture airtight. Let ferment in a warm area, between 77°F and 95°F (25°C and 35°C), until beverage turns effervescent (this will take from 3 to 10 days, depending on the temperature and concentration of ginger bug).

6. Refrigerate when the desired degree of effervescence is reached.

To be drunk in overalls after a hard day's work, with or without rum.

Both ginger beer and root beer keep for 3 months in the refrigerator.

Dried Aromatics Blend for Root Beer

Although they aren't very well known, all of the plants used to flavor root beer grow in the forests of North America and Europe. An herbalist can easily supply you with them. For this recipe, you will need the following dried herbs and spices:

¾ oz (20 g) sarsaparilla

¾ oz (20 g) wintergreen

½ oz (15 g) orange rind or 5 oz (150 g) fresh orange zest, without the pith (white part)

⅓ oz (10 g) sassafras root bark

½ tsp (2 mL) dandelion root

1 tsp (5 mL) burdock root, in pieces

1 tsp (5 mL) licorice root

1 cinnamon stick

1 star anise pod

LEVEL OF DIFFICULTY

TYPES OF FERMENTATION
Alcoholic (~5%) for cider;
acetic for vinegar

PREPARATION TIME
1 hour

FERMENTATION TIME
6 weeks

EQUIPMENT
Bowl, 1-gallon (4 L) carboy,
airlock, four 1-quart (1 L)
airtight glass bottles

FOR 16 CUPS (4 L) CIDER

¼ of a 1-g packet of
champagne yeast or
beer yeast

6 tbsp + 2 tsp (100 mL)
warm water

3 tsp (15 mL) cane sugar,
divided

16 cups (4 L) fresh,
unfiltered apple juice with
no preservatives

APPLE cider AND APPLE CIDER vinegar

1. Wash and sanitize equipment (see page 23).

2. In a bowl, activate yeast in warm water with 1 tsp (5 mL) sugar, or according to packet directions.

3. Pour apple juice into the carboy, then add activated yeast. Close carboy and set airlock.

4. Let ferment at 60°F to 71°F (16°C to 22°C) for 30 days or until bubbles are no longer visible in the airlock.

5. Let stand in the refrigerator for 24 hours to allow cider to settle; the yeast will sink to the bottom.

6. Sanitize bottles, then gently pour in cider, taking care not to stir up the yeast sediment. Discard solid residue.

7. Add ½ tsp (2 mL) sugar to each bottle, close and let ferment at room temperature for 2 weeks.

To consume during a friendly game of bocce.

Keeps for 2 months at room temperature or for 6 months in the refrigerator.

APPLE CIDER VINEGAR

If your cider doesn't smell nice or, worse, doesn't taste right, all is not lost: turn it into vinegar! Just replace the airlock on the carboy with breathable fabric, then forget the container in a corner of the house or attic for at least 6 months. That's all there is to it! Then you can start making marinades. If patience is not one of your virtues, add a few drops of unpasteurized vinegar to speed up the process. As in kombucha, a mother that is visible to the eye will form in the vinegar. It will serve to accelerate your future batches of vinegar. Many grandmothers confirm that apple cider vinegar is excellent for the digestion. All you need to do is swallow a tablespoonful before a meal. It is also an excellent remedy for the day after a night of drinking (this is one of the secrets of youth).

LEVEL OF DIFFICULTY

TYPE OF FERMENTATION
Alcoholic (~10%)

PREPARATION TIME
1 hour

FERMENTATION TIME
2 to 3 months + 2 weeks

EQUIPMENT
Bowls, 1-gallon (4 L) carboy, airlock, four 1-quart (1 L) airtight glass bottles

Mead

FOR 16 CUPS (4 L) MEAD

¼ of a 1-g packet of champagne yeast or beer yeast

6 tbsp + 2 tsp (100 mL) warm water

1 tsp (5 mL) cane sugar

4 cups (1 L) unpasteurized honey

12 cups (3 L) water, divided

1 tsp (5 mL) freshly squeezed lemon juice

2 tsp (10 mL) cane sugar (optional)

1. Wash and sanitize equipment (see page 23).
2. In a bowl, activate yeast in warm water with 1 tsp (5 mL) sugar, or according to package directions.
3. In another bowl, mix honey with 3 cups (750 mL) water until honey is dissolved and blended.
4. Pour honey mixture into the carboy. Add the remaining water and lemon juice, then activated yeast. Leave 1 inch (2.5 cm) of empty space in the neck of the carboy for the foam that will form during fermentation. If you do not, it will overflow. This isn't dangerous, but it will be sticky. Mix until consistency is uniform. Close carboy and set airlock.
5. Let ferment at 60°F to 71°F (16°C to 22°C) for 2 to 3 months or until bubbles are no longer visible in the airlock.
6. Let stand in the refrigerator for a few days to allow mead to settle; the yeast will sink to the bottom.
7. Sanitize bottles, then gently pour in mead, taking care not to stir up the yeast sediment. Discard solid residue.
8. For still mead, bottle and refrigerate. For sparkling mead with a kick, add ½ tsp (2 mL) sugar to each bottle, close and let ferment at room temperature for 2 weeks. Once mead is ready, refrigerate it.

To drink at a banquet, pretending you're a Viking.

Keeps for 2 months at room temperature or for 6 months in the refrigerator.

Dairy and Nondairy Milks

Because life WOULDN'T BE AS smooth WITHOUT THEM

THE IDEA OF KEEPING ANIMALS AS LIVESTOCK FOR THEIR MILK makes some of us uncomfortable about drinking it. For those of us at peace with the idea, remember that it's better fermented! Cow and goat milk may be nutritious, but they can be more difficult to digest. During the fermentation process, the bacteria that grow in cheese and yogurt digest the lactose for us (lactose is a sugar that many adults cannot digest). The fermentation process also expands the range of flavors we can enjoy!

Modern substitutes for animal milk have been gaining in popularity over the past few years — plant milks made from coconut, almonds, cashews, hemp, rice and, of course, soy. There are now a number of substitutes for cow and goat milk that allow us to reproduce many classic fermented milk products. In terms of variety, the fermentations made from these alternative milks cannot replace those offered by cow milk, but they do surpass their quality in some recipes. Kefir made from coconut milk is a finer product than kefir made from animal milk. Cheeses made from nuts, on the other hand, as delicious as they are, do not approach the flavor complexity of a good aged cheese made from raw animal milk.

In the pages that follow, you will find several recipes for fermentations that are easy to make and require almost no special equipment. For each classic dairy recipe, we've provided a vegan version to replace it. For those of you who wish to age their cheese for 36 months, we suggest you head to the farm, put on your straw hat and get serious.

DO I ALREADY HAVE WHAT I NEED IN THE FRIDGE?
Milk-based fermentations are typically made from a pure lactic acid bacteria culture (for example, yogurt) or from a mixed culture of

yeasts and lactic acid bacteria (for example, milk kefir). For vegan fermentations, miso and vegan yogurts such as Bio-K (some varieties are soy milk– or rice milk–based), as well as any unpasteurized nut yogurt, should contain the bacteria required to start your own culture.

For more traditional yogurts and cheeses, there are many brands of lactic starter culture sold in packets to add directly at the start of the fermentation process. Any supermarket yogurt or homemade yogurt can serve as a source of lactic acid bacteria to start your fermentations. The different kinds of lactobacteria dictate the variations in flavor and texture: one will produce thick yogurt, another a more liquid kefir and another, paired with rennet, will make a firm cheese.

HOW DOES IT WORK?

Lactic acid bacteria feed on sugar (lactose in animal milk, sucrose in plant milk) and mainly produce lactic acid, which helps protect milk from other harmful bacteria, thus prolonging its shelf life. Rennet is an enzyme that usually comes from the stomach of a calf (yes, you probably would have preferred not to know). Rennet solidifies milk.

Lactic ferments can be thermophilic (which means they thrive in heat) and survive well in temperatures around 108°F (42°C), or meso-philic (which means they like moderation) and prefer an environment of 86°F (30°C) or less. To put it more simply, the bacteria in yogurt love a heat wave, while the bacteria in milk kefir prefer air conditioning. For cheese, the type of bacteria varies according to the type of cheese being produced.

HOW DO I KNOW WHEN IT'S READY?

As with other fermentations, doneness is mainly a question of taste: we try a spoonful and, if we like it, we put it in the refrigerator. If it is bland, we let it be for a little while longer. Yogurt and kefir left to ferment too long will tend to separate (solids on top and liquids on the bottom, or vice versa). In this case, you can mix the product to make it smooth or simply add salt and drain it through cheesecloth. Then you can spread the solid product on a nice slice of bread and pretend you had planned all along to make cheese!

HOW DO I KNOW IF THERE ARE ONLY "GOOD" BACTERIA PARTYING IN MY JAR?

Vegetable lactofermentations in brine benefit from salt to keep away bad bacteria, but this is not the case for all dairy lactofermentations. Milk is an environment favorable to the growth of all kinds of bacteria, both harmful and good. So how do we make this work? The answer lies in the quantity of lactic acid bacteria we add at the start to ensure effective colonization of the environment, followed by quick acid-ification. The best guarantee of success: use tools that have been thoroughly washed (and even sanitized, at least the first few times you use the equipment), ferment at the right temperatures and use strong cultures — that is, cultures that are active and in sufficient quantities.

As it is quite obvious when milk has been infected with undesirable bacteria, a minimal amount of vigilance is often sufficient to detect the slightest anomaly. An unacceptable odor or the presence of pretty blue or green "blooms" will indicate that a step in the process did not follow its natural course.

ALMOND YOGURT (PAGE 106) AND
COW MILK YOGURT (PAGE 107)

LEVEL OF DIFFICULTY

TYPE OF FERMENTATION
Lactic

PREPARATION TIME
25 minutes

FERMENTATION TIME
6 to 12 hours

EQUIPMENT
Large bowl, blender, eight 8-oz (250 mL) glass jars, yogurt maker or dehydrator or oven; optional: fine-mesh sieve, bowl, cheesecloth and airtight container

ALMOND Yogurt
(VEGAN OR NOT)

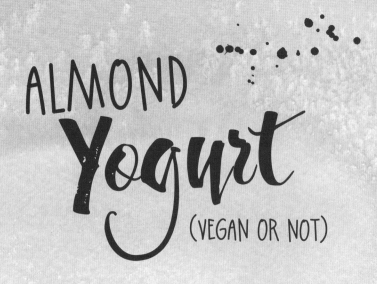

8 oz (250 g) raw almonds

8 oz (250 g) raw cashews (but don't worry if they're roasted)

4 cups (1 L) water

2 cups (500 mL) filtered water

3 tbsp (45 mL) honey

1 tsp (5 mL) active cow milk yogurt or vegan yogurt, or 1 packet yogurt starter culture

Pinch sea salt

1. In a large bowl, soak almonds and cashews in 4 cups (1 L) water for 8 hours. Drain nuts, then rinse with plenty of water.

2. In blender, purée almonds and cashews, 2 cups (500 mL) filtered water and honey until thick and creamy. Add yogurt (or culture) and salt, then blend for a few seconds.

3. Pour into jars, leaving about 1 inch (2.5 cm) of space on top, and seal airtight. Place in a yogurt maker, dehydrator or any other incubator (for example, the oven of an electric range, with heat off but oven light on) at 90°F to 104°F (32°C to 40°C). Let ferment for 6 to 8 hours.

4. Taste and, if needed, let ferment awhile longer for more pronounced flavor.

5. When yogurt is ready, shake jars to mix contents, then refrigerate.

6. For thicker yogurt, place a fine-mesh sieve over a bowl and line it with several layers of cheesecloth. Transfer yogurt to sieve and refrigerate for a few hours, until liquid has drained. Transfer yogurt to an airtight container.

TIP

If using yogurt starter culture, use the whole packet unless the instructions on the packet say otherwise.

LEVEL OF DIFFICULTY

TYPE OF FERMENTATION
Lactic

PREPARATION TIME
15 minutes

FERMENTATION TIME
6 to 12 hours

EQUIPMENT
12-cup (3 L) saucepan, thermometer, whisk, eight 8-oz (250 mL) glass jars, yogurt maker or dehydrator or oven; optional: fine-mesh sieve, bowl, cheesecloth and airtight container

Cow Milk YOGURT

> 8 cups (2 L) whole milk
>
> 1 packet yogurt starter culture or 3 tbsp (45 mL) active yogurt
>
> ½ tsp (2 g) sea salt

1. In the saucepan, heat milk over medium heat to 95°F to 104°F (35°C to 40°C).

2. Add yogurt culture (or active yogurt) and salt, then whisk until mixed.

3. Pour into jars, leaving about 1 inch (2.5 cm) of space on top, and seal airtight. Place in a yogurt maker, dehydrator or any other incubator (for example, the oven of an electric range, with heat off but oven light on) at 90°F to 104°F (32°C to 40°C). Let ferment for 6 to 8 hours.

4. Taste and, if needed, let ferment awhile longer for more pronounced flavor.

5. When yogurt is ready, shake jars to mix contents, then refrigerate.

6. For thicker yogurt, place a fine-mesh sieve over a bowl and line it with several layers of cheesecloth. Transfer yogurt to sieve and refrigerate for a few hours, until liquid has drained. Transfer yogurt to an airtight container.

Serve in verrines or dessert cups, over homemade jam, pomegranate seeds, puréed fresh figs or a little wild honey from the beehives of your brother-in-law the beekeeper up north.

Both Almond Yogurt and Cow Milk Yogurt will keep for 2 weeks in the refrigerator.

> Everyone dreams of the perfect yogurt: as creamy as can be without being too rich, not too liquid, with a fresh taste that is not too acidic, and just sweet enough to accompany perfectly ripe fruit. Few are willing to take matters into their own hands. Making yogurt is child's play and much more economical than buying it at your local grocery store. Tired of the usual? Try the almond yogurt — guaranteed to please!

LEVEL OF DIFFICULTY

TYPE OF FERMENTATION
Lactic

PREPARATION TIME
10 minutes

FERMENTATION TIME
12 to 24 hours

EQUIPMENT
2-quart (2 L) jar, breathable fabric, elastic band or string, fine-mesh sieve or cheesecloth, blender (optional)

1 cup (180 g) active milk kefir grains or 1 packet milk kefir powder

2 cans (each 14 oz/400 mL) coconut milk and ¾ cup + 2 tbsp (200 mL) water, or 4 cups (1 L) coconut milk from a carton (the best choice for this recipe), or whole cow or goat milk (not as good a choice for this recipe)

2 tbsp (25 g) cane sugar

½ tsp (2 mL) agar-agar (optional)

6 tbsp + 2 tsp (100 mL) boiling water (optional)

milk kefir
(COCONUT, COW OR GOAT)

1. Clean and sanitize equipment (see page 23).

2. Place kefir grains in the jar. Add milk (and water, if using), then sugar. Shake gently to mix.

3. Cover mouth of jar with fabric that allows air (but not insects) to pass through and attach with an elastic band or string. Let ferment out of direct light at room temperature (preferably 75°F/24°C) for 12 to 16 hours.

4. Taste kefir — it should be slightly acidic and effervescent. If necessary, let ferment for a few more hours.

5. Pour kefir through a fine-mesh sieve or cheesecloth into a bowl, then preserve grains in a jar, with enough milk to keep them submerged, in the refrigerator until the next use.

6. For thicker kefir, dissolve agar-agar in boiling water. Add this mixture, while still hot, to filtered fermented kefir, mix well and refrigerate for 1 hour.

7. When kefir has set, purée in blender until creamy. (This option is also applicable to other yogurts.)

Use kefir as you would use yogurt (with granola, in sauces, etc.) or drink it! It's amazing in a smoothie or a milkshake (page 187). To reduce the acidic flavor, it can be cut with milk just before drinking.

Keeps for 1 week in the refrigerator. The grains can be kept for a lifetime, as long as less than 6 weeks elapse between uses.

Q&A

1. What is the difference between kefir grains and kefir powder?
See Water Kefir, page 84.

2. What is the difference between water kefir grains and milk kefir grains? *Kefir grains have a short memory: they quickly "forget" how to digest lactose, a complex carbohydrate, after they have fermented simpler sugars like glucose and fructose, which are found in fruit and in cane sugar. A milk kefir strain is therefore more flexible in what it is able to ferment. If you wish to preserve wild grains that are ferocious toward lactose, you should feed them with milk between each nondairy fermentation (if you are vegan, feed them with coconut milk). That way, you will have more bacterial power at hand to invade and populate your internal continents.*

3. I forgot to use my grains for several weeks. Are they ruined?
Probably not, but they will be sleepier and less effective. You'll have to try them and hope for the best, making sure to produce only small quantities of kefir at a time.

Milk kefir has a flavor very similar to yogurt, but it is more liquid and slightly effervescent. It contains many more varied strains of probiotics and colonizing bacteria (bacteria that settle in the gut and proliferate there, as opposed to transitory bacteria, which are useful only during their passage through the gut). Coconut milk, which does not contain lactose, ferments just as well with water kefir grains as with milk kefir grains. On the other hand, only milk kefir grains can ferment animal milk.

This classic creation of David's has proven its worth at his restaurant, with customers fighting over the last spoonfuls at the end of the day. It's a vegan version of cream cheese that is out of this world, with no aftertaste. Bring on the bread!

CASHEW
Labneh WITH
za'atar

TYPE OF FERMENTATION
Lactic

PREPARATION TIME
10 minutes

FERMENTATION TIME
6 to 10 hours

EQUIPMENT
Coffee grinder or mortar
and pestle, blender or food
processor, three 8-oz (250 mL)
glass jars, yogurt maker or
dehydrator or oven, fine-mesh
sieve, bowl, cheesecloth,
airtight container

ZA'ATAR

2 tbsp (30 mL) dried savory

2 tbsp (30 mL) dried
oregano

2 tbsp (30 mL) dried thyme

1 tbsp (15 mL) dried sumac

¼ cup (60 mL) toasted
sesame seeds

LABNEH

1⅔ cups (250 g) raw
cashews or pine nuts, or
sunflower seeds if the
budget is tight this month

Za'atar to taste

½ tsp (2 g) salt

1 cup (250 mL) water
(approx.)

½ tsp (2 mL) Miso (page 148)
or 1 packet yogurt starter
culture

ZA'ATAR

1. Grind savory, oregano, thyme, sumac and sesame seeds in a coffee
    grinder or crush with a mortar and pestle (or just buy za'atar spice
    blend at the supermarket).

LABNEH

1. Sanitize blender or food processor, equipment and glass jars by
    pouring in a little boiling water and letting stand for 2 minutes or
    using a sanitizing solution (see page 23).

2. In blender or food processor, combine cashews, za'atar to taste,
    salt, water and miso; purée into a smooth paste. Add more water
    if needed.

3. Transfer mixture to jars and seal airtight. Place in a yogurt maker,
    dehydrator or any other incubator (for example, the oven of an
    electric range, with heat off but oven light on) at 90°F to 104°F
    (32°C to 40°C). Let ferment for 6 to 8 hours.

4. Taste and, if needed, let ferment for another 1 to 2 hours for a
    more pronounced flavor.

5. Place a fine-mesh sieve over a bowl and line it with several layers
    of cheesecloth. Transfer labneh to sieve and refrigerate for a
    few hours, until liquid has drained. Transfer labneh to an airtight
    container. You now have lactose-free labneh.

Out of this world on fresh naan (page 121) with za'atar.

Keeps for 1 week in the refrigerator.

TIP

*If using yogurt starter culture, use the whole packet unless the
instructions on the packet say otherwise.*

TYPE OF FERMENTATION
Lactic

PREPARATION TIME
10 minutes

FERMENTATION TIME
8 hours

EQUIPMENT
16-cup (4 L) pot, thermometer, dehydrator or oven, strainer, cheesecloth, 2 plates, airtight container

16 cups (4 L) whole milk, unhomogenized if possible

1 packet cheese or yogurt starter culture or 2 tbsp (30 mL) fresh cheese or yogurt

¼ rennet tablet (sometimes life is complicated)

3 tsp (15 g) sea salt, or to taste

HOMEMADE
Cheese Spread

1. In the large pot, heat milk over medium heat to 95°F to 104°F (35°C to 40°C).

2. Add starter culture, then rennet. Mix together. Cover and let stand for 4 hours, without stirring.

3. Place covered pot in dehydrator or another incubator (for example, the oven of an electric range, with heat off but oven light on) at 90°F to 104°F (32°C to 40°C). Let ferment for 4 hours. The milk should be solidified and the unmistakable aroma of cheese should be apparent. To check, scoop up a spoonful; the curd should maintain its shape on the spoon.

4. Using a knife, cut solidified curd into cubes, like a chessboard. Let stand for 15 minutes. Stir very gently without breaking pieces, then let stand for another 15 minutes.

5. Transfer cheese to a strainer lined with cheesecloth and let whey drain off for 30 minutes. Add salt to taste, stirring to blend.

6. Make a knot in cheesecloth to form a bundle. Press down a little with your hands to release whey. Transfer bundle to a plate and lay another plate on top as a weight. Refrigerate for 3 hours.

7. Transfer solids to an airtight container and mix until texture is uniform.

Spread generously on one (or several) wood oven–baked Montreal bagels.

Keeps for 2 weeks in the refrigerator.

No cheese is easier to master. You'll regret that it took you so long to try your hand at making it! (For a vegan version, see Cashew Labneh with Za'atar, page 111.)

Grains
and Legumes

Bread, SAKE and everything in between

MAKING BREAD IS A SOURCE OF HAPPINESS. Kneading dough is a good way to unwind and relax after a stressful day. The historical foundations of fermentation are based on wheat (in the West) and rice (in the East). Without these two grains, a good many celebrations since the dawn of mankind would have fallen flat.

Grains and legumes are fairly close in terms of appearance and use in cooking. Legumes, however, represent a source of protein, while grains are mainly a source of carbohydrates. Another marked difference, especially in our time: many grains, particularly wheat, contain gluten, a succulent protein with which we have a love-hate relationship. In this chapter, you will find traditional recipes that include gluten, as well as gluten-free substitutes. The recipes are divided into three categories: bread, alcoholic beverages and grains fermented with mold.

BREAD (IN ALL ITS FORMS)
Wheat Flours

All-purpose flour and bread flour are the best for making bread because they contain a lot of gluten. Gluten gives dough its elasticity. During the kneading process, wheat gluten forms what we call a gluten "network." These flexible links keep gases and moisture in the bread, helping it rise. Whole-grain and whole wheat flours also contain bran. Although bran is very nutritious, it makes the job more difficult for the gluten by "cutting into" its network. That is why bread made with bran does not rise as easily as bread made without bran. Mixing all-purpose flour and whole wheat flour in equal parts is a good compromise, producing bread that is both tasty and nutritious. Once you have mastered whole wheat bread, you are free to explore the different types of flour and what they have to offer.

Gluten-Free Flours

Making a good loaf of bread using gluten-free flour is a considerable feat that seems almost impossible. The moisture in the grains before they are ground, the proportions of the flours mixed together (because it won't work to use only one kind of gluten-free flour), the temperature of the oven for baking, even the weather on the day of making the bread seem to influence the final results, which can be a big letdown. On page 129, however, you'll find a gluten-free bread recipe that really works! To achieve this, we use flours that have been mixed and prepared with care by gluten-free professionals (see tip, page 129). We wish you good luck in this undertaking.

If gluten is not a problem for you, there is no need to skip any of our recipes. It should be noted that bread that contains gluten but is made from a sourdough starter is often more easily tolerated by those who are slightly sensitive to gluten. This is because the fermentation in the sourdough produces enzymes that facilitate digestion.

Salt

Salt, specifically sea salt, is an element that should not be left out of any type of rising dough. It helps gluten form and makes bread taste better. Salt "phobia" is probably the most common cause of mediocre bread — so go ahead and add your grain of salt.

Sourdough Starter or Yeast?

Sourdough starter (page 118) is a dough fermented by a variety of bacteria and wild yeasts that are present on the grains and in the environment, and which have spontaneously adopted the dough as a permanent home. The lactic acid bacteria in this mixed (lactic and alcoholic) fermentation give sourdough bread its slightly acidic characteristic. Dough with a sourdough base will take longer to rise than dough made with commercial yeast, but this investment in time and patience will reward you with a wealth and complexity of flavors, and bread that is easier to digest.

Even though sourdough is generally judged to be superior in flavor, we don't always have a sourdough starter on hand. A good baker's yeast (bread yeast) will do the job just fine. This more commercial yeast will produce only alcoholic fermentation. It is sold as a brick or cube (active fresh yeast) or in a packet (dry yeast to be reactivated in warm water). Like the yeasts in sourdough, baker's yeast feeds on sugars that are present in the flour, then releases carbon dioxide. Imprisoned in the dough, this carbon dioxide gives bread its characteristic bubbles and releases the classic fresh-bread aroma that instantly evokes a hundred happy memories.

ALCOHOLIC BEVERAGES

For liquid alcoholic fermentations, the secret of success lies in two things:

1. Maintaining a temperature of 59°F to 77°F (15°C to 25°C) (lower for sake, higher for homemade beer);
2. An oxygen-free (anaerobic) environment.

You read this correctly: exposure to the air is to be avoided at all costs. During the fermentation process, it's very tempting to remove a small sample so you can taste and judge how the product is evolving. It's also the best way to ruin it! In fermentation, keep in mind that the yeasts suspended in an alcoholic beverage that give it a milky appearance will also produce a more bitter flavor. To avoid unnecessary disappointment, it's better to wait until the fermentation is complete and for the yeasts to settle before tasting. While waiting for the big day, bide your time and go buy a beer at your local store.

FERMENTATIONS WITH MOLDS

Legume fermentations are often mold-based, but grains can also undergo this kind of transformation. The keys to success when fermenting with mold are:

1. A high moisture level: a moist environment is necessary for the development of molds, but not to the point of causing condensation. It is normal for a moist, hot environment to produce a little condensation, but if droplets of water start to form and wet the product, the growth of mold will slow down and bacteria will move in and throw a party. In the same way, a bean that is overcooked and turned into paste, or rice cooked in water instead of steam, will produce products that are too moist and that risk having bacteria take over.

2. A temperature maintained between 82°F and 95°F (between 28°C and 35°C).

3. Good aeration: mold needs to breathe, a lot more than we realize. Plastic containers and plastic bags must therefore have holes in them.

To know if a fermentation has gone well, trust your nose: if it smells strongly of "feet" or "seafood," or if you can discern wet or sticky traces where mold has not developed, it's better to start over again. On the other hand, the aromas that attest to the success of a fermentation are faint, unique and pleasing: koji smells acidic and like vanilla; tempeh has an aroma that is slightly sweet.

TYPES OF FERMENTATION
Lactic, alcoholic

PREPARATION TIME
5 minutes per day for 5 days

FERMENTATION TIME
3 to 5 days, then continuous, fed at 24-hour intervals

EQUIPMENT
4-cup (1 L) bowl, plate to cover bowl

Sourdough STARTER

QUANTITIES NEEDED EACH DAY

¼ cup (30 g) whole wheat or rye flour

⅓ cup + 2 tsp (85 mL) water

1. In the bowl, mix flour and water (the mixture will be liquid). Cover bowl with a plate and store in a warm area (82°F to 95°F/28°C to 35°C) for 24 hours.

2. Discard half the volume of the sourdough (see tip) — to avoid making a mountain of it with increasingly larger additions — and add the same quantity of flour and water to the sourdough as the day before. Mix, cover bowl with plate and let rest again.

3. Repeat step 2 at 24-hour intervals.

4. After 3 to 5 days, the sourdough will produce a lot of bubbles in a continuous fashion. It is ready to be used.

Sourdough produces delicious breads (see Country-Style Miche, page 125; Naan, page 121) and crêpes (see Dosas, page 122). In some recipes (see Fermented Banana Bread, page 126), it can replace yeast and even baking powder.

You can grow sourdough indefinitely by continuing to feed it every 24 hours. In this case, double the amount of flour and water added each day. For example, on Day 1, add ¼ cup (30 g) flour and ⅓ cup + 2 tsp (85 mL) water; on Day 2, add ½ cup (60 g) flour and ⅔ cup + 4 tsp (170 mL) water; on Day 3, add 1 cup (120 g) flour and 1⅓ cups + 1 tbsp (340 mL) water; and so on.

To put your sourdough "on hold" for up to 1 month between uses, store it in the refrigerator. To revive, discard half, feed the remainder with flour and water and let stand for 24 hours before use.

TIP

If you don't want to throw away any portion of this treasure (we understand; we don't like the idea either), make yourself a crêpe! This will help you judge if the mixture is to your taste.

Working your sourdough is an art that turns into an obsession for some bakers. Sourdough needs tender loving care: you have to provide it with a home for some time and care for it every day! To start a sourdough, we always use whole rye or wheat flour, which contain more microorganisms than all-purpose flours. We understand the attraction of watching your own sourdough being born, but we still recommend that you try to find some already living in your community (from your local bakery or among your acquaintances). Domesticating it will be simple. Through experimentation, you will eventually "know" the ideal sourdough for your tastes and be able to play with the parameters of temperature, moisture and maintenance to adjust its acidity level.

Every nationality has its flatbread: Italians have piadina and pizza; Greeks have pitas; Iranians have barbari bread; Mexicans have tortillas; and Indians have their fabulous naan. This basic recipe can be adapted to make any kind of flatbread you've been fantasizing about.

LEVEL OF DIFFICULTY

TYPE OF FERMENTATION
Alcoholic (yes, alcoholic!)

PREPARATION TIME
30 minutes

FERMENTATION TIME
1 to 3 hours

EQUIPMENT
12-cup (3 L) bowl, plate to cover bowl, baking sheet, tandoori oven (in the perfect world!) or wood fire or barbecue or skillet…, clean cloth

Naan

FOR 6 NAAN

¼ cup (60 mL) Sourdough Starter (page 118) and ¾ cup + 2 tbsp (200 mL) warm water (<86°F/30°C), or 1 packet (5 g) active dry bread yeast and 1 cup (250 mL) warm water (<86°F/30°C)

2 tbsp (30 mL) plain yogurt (page 107)

1¾ cups (240 g) all-purpose flour (approx.)

2 tsp (10 g) salt (important!)

1. In the bowl, mix sourdough starter (or yeast), water and yogurt. Let stand for 10 minutes.

2. Add flour, then mix with a fork for 1 minute. Let stand at room temperature for 30 minutes.

3. Add salt, then mix. If needed, add water or flour to make dough flexible and just slightly sticky. Knead dough with your hands, in the bowl, for 5 minutes. Cover bowl with a plate and let stand in a warm area (80°F to 98°F/27°C to 37°C) for 1 to 3 hours or until dough has doubled in volume.

4. Knead dough gently for 2 minutes, then separate into 6 balls. Flatten balls by hand or with rolling pin, sprinkling flour on dough to prevent balls from sticking. Place balls on a baking sheet and let stand for 15 minutes.

5. Bake at very high heat (500°F/260°C), on a hot stone, on a barbecue or in a skillet, for 1 minute on each side.

6. Remove from heat and cover with a clean cloth to hold in some of the steam and prevent naan from drying out.

To eat hot while watching a Bollywood film.

Keeps for 5 days in an airtight container at room temperature.

LEVEL OF DIFFICULTY

TYPES OF FERMENTATION
Alcoholic, lactic

PREPARATION TIME
1 hour + 6 hours soaking time

FERMENTATION TIME
8 to 12 hours

EQUIPMENT
Bowls, blender

Dosas

(SAVORY LENTIL CRÊPES)

FOR 12 SMALL CRÊPES

2 cups (400 g) white or brown rice, or 2½ cups (400 g) rice flour

1 cup (220 g) split dried green or black lentils, or 1¾ cups (220 g) lentil flour

Filtered water

½ tsp (2 mL) fenugreek seeds

1 tsp (5 g) salt

1 tbsp (15 mL) Sourdough Starter (page 118), or let wild fermentation do its thing!

1 tsp (5 mL) butter (or ghee) or coconut oil, softened or melted

A tiny amount of olive oil

1. Place rice in a bowl and lentils in another bowl. Cover each with filtered water and soak for 6 hours. Take a nap during this time. (If using flours instead of rice and lentils, go directly to step 4.)

2. Drain lentils. In a blender, process lentils with ½ cup (125 mL) filtered water until they are thoroughly cracked but not perfectly smooth. Pour into a large bowl and set aside.

3. Drain rice. In blender, purée rice with 1 cup (250 mL) filtered water until almost smooth.

4. Add rice to lentil mixture. (Or combine rice flour, lentil flour and 2⅓ cups + 5 tsp/600 mL filtered water.) Stir in fenugreek seeds, salt, sourdough starter and butter. The consistency should be that of crêpe batter. If batter is too thick, add a little filtered water.

5. Cover with a plate or plastic wrap and let ferment in a hot area (between 80°F and 98°F/27°C and 37°C) for 8 to 12 hours, depending on the temperature and starter culture used. Mixture is ready when you can see a lot of bubbles and can unequivocally state: "Wow! It's moving!" At this stage, the batter can be kept in the refrigerator for 2 days, but it is best if used immediately.

6. Heat a lightly oiled skillet over high heat. Pour in 1 tbsp (15 mL) batter, then quickly spread batter to obtain a very thin crêpe. Cook for 1 minute on each side or until crêpe is crispy and golden. Repeat with the remaining batter until all crêpes are cooked.

To be eaten with yogurt (page 107) and herbs, or labneh (page 111) and a nice chutney (page 68), or soaked in maple syrup like there's no tomorrow...

Keeps for 3 days in the refrigerator.

TIP

It is possible to use spontaneous fermentation for this recipe, which means trusting the action of ambient wild yeasts and omitting the sourdough starter. The success rate is higher if the ambient temperature is high.

Making a nice loaf of sourdough bread is the best way to get in someone's good graces. *Panem et circenses* (bread and circuses) was the Roman emperors' strategy for appeasing the people and preventing a rebellion. In our experience, it still works. Present a loaf of homemade bread to the one you love, and you'll capture their heart.

Country-Style Miche

TYPES OF FERMENTATION
Alcoholic, lactic (if made with sourdough)

PREPARATION TIME
30 minutes + 1 hour baking

FERMENTATION TIME
3 to 4 hours for yeast; 6 to 9 hours for sourdough

EQUIPMENT
12-cup (3 L) bowl, 12-cup (3 L) large ovenproof pot with lid (see tip), well-sharpened knife

½ cup (125 mL) Sourdough Starter (page 118) and 1⅓ cups + 1 tbsp (340 mL) warm water, or 1 packet (5 g) bread yeast and 6 tbsp + 2 tsp (100 mL) warm water

7 tbsp (60 g) whole wheat flour

2⅔ cups (360 g) all-purpose flour (approx.), divided

2 tsp (10 g) sea salt

2 tsp (10 mL) cane sugar

2 tsp (10 mL) cornmeal or 1 tsp (5 mL) flour to sprinkle in pot

TIP

If you don't have a large pot, place the dough in a loaf pan, preferably one with a lid to hold in the steam. This will help the bread form a nice crust. If you don't have a lid, toss 5 or 6 ice cubes into a pan in the oven 30 seconds before putting in the bread. The ice cubes will melt in the first few minutes of baking and produce the steam you need for a nice crust.

1. If using sourdough starter, mix with water in a large bowl. If using yeast, activate in bowl according to directions on package.

2. Add whole wheat flour and 2 cups + 7 tbsp (330 g) all-purpose flour. Mix with a fork for 1 minute and let stand for 30 minutes to allow flour to absorb water.

3. Add salt and sugar. Mix with a fork until mixture forms a ball that is flexible but not too sticky. Add more flour if dough is too sticky.

4. Once desired texture is achieved, knead dough in bowl or on a floured work surface, using your fists: push your fists down in center of dough, then fold in sides. Knead for 5 minutes.

5. Return dough to bowl, if necessary. Cover with a damp cloth or plastic wrap and let stand in a warm area (80°F to 98°F/27°C to 37°C; for example, the oven of an electric range, with heat off but oven light on) until dough has almost doubled in volume (1 to 2 hours for yeast, 3 to 6 hours for sourdough).

6. Knead dough for 1 minute, then form into a ball again. Cover with damp cloth or plastic wrap and let rise in a warm area for 1 hour if using yeast or 2 hours if using sourdough.

7. Place the empty large pot with lid in the oven and preheat at 425°F (220°C) for 30 minutes.

8. When dough has expanded to a satisfactory size, remove pot from oven, remove lid and sprinkle cornmeal or flour inside. Place dough in pot. Using a well-sharpened knife, make a few incisions on the loaf: slide the tip of the knife across the surface of the dough, without exerting pressure, to "sign" the crust. Cover pot and return to oven.

9. Bake for 30 minutes. Reduce temperature to 350°F (180°C), remove lid and bake for another 30 minutes or until crust is golden (you should hear a hollow thud, characteristic of baked bread, when you gently tap the crust).

10. Remove from oven and let cool on a rack. Wait 1 more hour before tasting. The interior will continue to bake as long as the bread is warm.

To eat with olive oil before, during and after a meal.

Keeps for 5 days in an airtight container at room temperature.

LEVEL OF DIFFICULTY

TYPE OF FERMENTATION
Alcoholic

PREPARATION TIME
20 minutes + 45 minutes baking

FERMENTATION TIME
1½ hours for yeast; 2 to 3 hours for sourdough

EQUIPMENT
10- by 3-inch (25 by 8 cm) loaf pan, two 8-cup (2 L) bowls, damp cloth

¼ cup (60 mL) Sourdough Starter (page 118), or
1 packet (5 g) bread yeast + ¼ cup (60 mL) warm water

2 cups (270 g) all-purpose flour

1 cup (210 g) packed brown sugar

½ tsp (2 g) salt

3 very ripe bananas, mashed with a fork

2 large eggs (see tip)

⅓ cup + 2 tsp (85 mL) plain yogurt or nut yogurt

¼ cup (60 mL) coconut oil

1 tsp (5 mL) vanilla extract

FERMENTED
banana bread

1. Grease loaf pan and sprinkle with flour.

2. If using yeast, follow directions on package to activate.

3. In a large bowl, combine flour, sugar and salt.

4. In another bowl, whisk together sourdough starter (or activated yeast), bananas, eggs, yogurt, coconut oil and vanilla.

5. Pour liquid mixture over dry ingredients and mix until dough is of uniform consistency.

6. Transfer dough to loaf pan, cover with a damp cloth and let stand in a warm area (80°F to 98°F/27°C to 37°C) until it expands by 50% (about 1½ hours for yeast, 2 to 3 hours for sourdough).

7. Preheat oven to 350°F (180°C).

8. Bake for 45 minutes or until a tester inserted in the center of the loaf comes out clean. Let stand for 30 minutes before serving.

To eat with warm thoughts of your grandmother.

Keeps in an airtight container at room temperature for 5 days or, sliced and individually wrapped in plastic wrap, in the freezer for 6 months. Heat in the toaster and spread coconut butter on top.

TIP

For a vegan version, simply replace the eggs with 3 tbsp (45 mL) ground chia seeds mixed with ½ cup (125 mL) water.

This recipe is a fermented variation of Sébastien's mother's banana bread, traditionally made with baking powder. We reworked the recipe to make the bread rise by fermenting it, and the result is really delicious. A cake that rises through fermentation will be more sensitive to environmental factors: it may rise high and have a domed top, or it may be slightly collapsed. Don't be prejudiced toward the latter — it will be just as delicious!

LEVEL OF DIFFICULTY

TYPE OF FERMENTATION
Alcoholic

PREPARATION TIME
25 minutes + 1 hour baking

FERMENTATION TIME
1 hour, 40 minutes

EQUIPMENT
Thermometer, coffee grinder, 8-cup (2 L) bowl (optional), electric handheld mixer or stand mixer fitted with a flat paddle, damp cloth, oiled 7-inch (18 cm) glass baking dish

2 tbsp (20 g) flax seeds

2 tbsp (24 g) chia seeds

1¾ cups + 2 tbsp (280 g) gluten-free flour (see tip)

½ cup (70 g) sorghum flour

¾ tsp (3 g) sea salt

1 tsp (5 mL) instant (quick-rising) yeast

1½ cups (375 mL) water, heated to 113°F (45°C)

2 tbsp (30 mL) olive oil

2 tbsp (30 mL) pure maple syrup

3 tbsp (30 g) hemp seeds + more to sprinkle

GLUTEN-FREE
Sorghum and
Hemp
COUNTRY—STYLE BREAD*

1. In a coffee grinder, finely grind flax seeds, then chia seeds.

2. In a large bowl (or in bowl of stand mixer), combine ground flax seeds and chia seeds, gluten-free flour, sorghum flour, salt and yeast.

3. Add water, oil and maple syrup. Using an electric mixer, vigorously beat mixture on medium speed for about 2 minutes (maybe 3 minutes if you're not in a hurry).

4. Cover bowl with a damp cloth and let stand at room temperature in a draft-free place for 60 minutes. Have a bath and, when you return, stir with a wooden spoon.

5. Add 3 tbsp (30 g) hemp seeds and stir again.

6. Cover bottom and sides of oiled baking dish with hemp seeds (important to prevent bread from sticking to dish and to make it easier to remove).

7. Transfer dough to baking dish and spread evenly with a wet spatula. Sprinkle with hemp seeds to taste.

8. Place on middle rack in oven, with heat off and oven light on. Let rise for 30 to 40 minutes. The bread will be ready to bake when a finger pressed down lightly on the surface leaves a print (it will no longer bounce back after it is touched).

9. Without removing bread from oven, set oven to 350°F (180°C). Bake for about 1 hour or until golden brown. Remove from baking dish and let cool on a rack.

If all has gone well, slice and enjoy; if not, use as a carving stone.

Keeps for 5 days in an airtight container at room temperature.

TIP

We use La Merveilleuse brand flour (from Cuisine l'Angélique), which yields the best results for gluten-free bread. If it's not available, look for a gluten-free flour blend that contains a mixture of unrefined flours, starch, flax seeds, baking powder, guar gum and xanthan gum.

* This recipe was created by Caroline Roy of Cuisine l'Angélique for this book.

LEVEL OF DIFFICULTY

TYPE OF FERMENTATION
Alcoholic (~6%)

PREPARATION TIME
3 hours

FERMENTATION TIME
21 days

EQUIPMENT
Scale, 16-cup (4 L) stainless steel pot with lid, cotton brewing bag or cheesecloth, 1-gallon (4 L) bucket with lid or 1¼-gallon (5 L) carboy, airlock, four 1-quart (1 L) airtight glass bottles

FOR 16 CUPS (4 L)

2 lb 3 oz (1 kg) malt extract

6 cups (1.5 L) filtered water

½ cup (5 g) dry bittering hops

6 cups (1.5 L) cold filtered water

1 packet (5 g) dry beer yeast (see Where to Buy This Strange Stuff, page 197)

2 tsp (10 mL) granulated or raw cane sugar

Beer

1. Wash and sanitize all containers and instruments (see page 23).

2. In a large pot, add malt extract to 6 cups (1.5 L) filtered water and mix thoroughly. Bring to a boil over high heat.

3. Place hops in the brewing bag or on cheesecloth, bundle and tie in a knot. Add to pot and steep in boiling water for 30 minutes (maintain a boil, but watch that it doesn't boil over). Remove from heat. Remove hops and add them to your compost.

4. Add 6 cups (1.5 L) cold water to mixture to cool it down to between 65°F and 77°F (18°C and 25°C).

5. Oxygenate mixture by shaking pot vigorously to produce bubbles.

6. Use a sanitized instrument to stir in yeast. Transfer mixture to bucket. Seal airtight and set airlock. Let ferment at 68°F to 77°F (20°C to 25°C) for 6 days or until mixture no longer produces bubbles.

7. Refrigerate bucket (under 50°F/10°C) for 24 hours, until beer settles.

8. Carefully pour beer (without raising sediment) into sanitized bottles. Add ½ tsp (2 mL) sugar to each bottle before sealing. Let ferment in a warm area (77°F to 90°F/25°C to 32°C) for 14 days, then refrigerate.

To consume when necessary — that is to say, on days of rest and after a long, hard day's work.

Keeps for 1 month in the refrigerator (if well hidden from others!).

The beer purity laws established in Europe in the 1500s limited beer ingredients to water, hops and malt. This is a very conventional recipe that respects the puritanical nature of traditional brewing. On the other hand, if you allow a few cocoa beans or raspberry leaves, or a bit of honey, to fall into the brew, it will not be held against you.

The Miracle of Beer

Beer comes from barley grains that are soaked, sprouted, roasted and then dried to produce malt. Malting helps create the enzymes needed to transform the starch in the grains into simpler sugars. Roasting and blending grains from different roasts is an art that brewers constantly strive to perfect, as this influences alcohol content, flavor, color and residual sugars. If you want to avoid the complexity of this stage, the best way to begin making beer of any kind is to buy a malt extract beer kit. These kits help reduce the number of tools and amount of expertise you will need for home brewing.

Braggot (sometimes called bracket) is a fermented alcohol made from the sugars in honey and malt. In place of hops, a mixture of herbs and fruit is used. The possibilities are endless, so feel free to express yourself! If your creativity yields less than satisfactory results, you can always make a nice vinegar...

TYPE OF FERMENTATION
Alcoholic (~6%)

PREPARATION TIME
3 hours

FERMENTATION TIME
21 days

EQUIPMENT
Scale, 16-cup (4 L) stainless steel pot with lid, cotton brewing bag or cheesecloth, thermometer, 1¼-gallon (5 L) carboy, airlock, four 1-quart (1 L) resealable glass bottles

FOR 16 CUPS (4 L)

18 oz (500 g) malt extract

6 cups (1.5 L) filtered water

9 oz (250 g) berries (your choice, according to season)

1 bunch fresh herbs (mint, lemon verbena, lemongrass, basil or hop's cousin, hemp)

18 oz (500 g) pasteurized honey

2 tsp (10 mL) freshly squeezed lemon juice

6 cups (1.5 L) cold filtered water

1 packet (5 g) dry beer yeast (see Where to Buy This Strange Stuff, page 197)

2 tsp (10 mL) granulated or raw cane sugar

Braggot

1. Wash and sanitize all containers and instruments (see page 23).

2. In a large pot, add malt extract to 6 cups (1.5 L) filtered water and mix thoroughly. Bring to a boil over high heat.

3. Place berries and herbs in the brewing bag or on cheesecloth, bundle and tie in a knot. Add to pot with honey and lemon juice; steep in boiling water for 30 minutes (maintain a boil, but watch that it doesn't boil over). Remove from heat. Remove bundle of fruit and herbs.

4. Add 6 cups (1.5 L) cold water to mixture to cool it down to between 65°F and 77°F (18°C and 25°C).

5. Use a sanitized instrument to stir in yeast. Transfer mixture to carboy. Seal airtight and set airlock. Let ferment at 68°F to 77°F (20°F to 25°C) for 6 days or until mixture no longer produces bubbles.

6. Refrigerate carboy (under 50°F/10°C) for 24 hours, until braggot settles.

7. Carefully pour braggot (without raising sediment) into sanitized bottles. Add ½ tsp (2 mL) sugar to each bottle before sealing. Let ferment in a warm area (77°F to 90°F/25°C to 32°C) for 14 days, then refrigerate or store at room temperature.

Irresistible with a chocolate dessert or seitan jerky (page 137).

Keeps for 3 months in the refrigerator or 1 month at room temperature.

Tempeh

LEVEL OF DIFFICULTY

TYPES OF FERMENTATION
Proteolytic, mold (*Rhizopus oligosporus, Rhizopus orizae*)

PREPARATION TIME
2 hours + 12 hours soaking time

FERMENTATION TIME
24 to 36 hours

EQUIPMENT
Scale, bowls, 16-cup (4 L) pot, baking sheet, 4 to 5 small resealable freezer bags, incubator

18 oz (500 g) dried soybeans, fava beans or other dried legumes

Water

1 tbsp (15 mL) white vinegar, apple cider vinegar or freshly squeezed lemon juice

1 tsp (5 mL) tempeh starter culture (see Where to Buy This Strange Stuff, page 197)

1. In a large bowl, soak beans in enough water to cover for 12 hours. Drain, rinse and remove outer skins, if needed (for fava beans).

2. In a large pot, combine beans, 12 cups (3 L) fresh water and vinegar; cook over medium heat for 30 minutes or until beans are tender.

3. Drain beans, then spread on a baking sheet. Let stand until temperature drops to 104°F (40°C) and beans are completely dry on the surface.

4. Transfer beans to a bowl and sprinkle starter culture on top. Mix with a spoon for at least 1 minute to distribute spores evenly.

5. Place freezer bags on a cutting board. Using the tip of a small sharpened knife, perforate bags with tiny holes spaced 1/2 inch (1 cm) apart. This will allow tempeh to breathe. The holes must be as small as possible, because too much air will encourage black spores to appear (not dangerous, but not appetizing, either). However, if there are not enough holes, tempeh will have difficulty growing.

6. Divide beans among freezer bags and gently flatten to a thickness of 3/4 to 1 1/4 inch (2 to 3 cm) to eliminate air pockets.

7. Place in an incubator, such as a dehydrator (see tip) or the oven of an electric range, with heat off but oven light on, at 82°F to 93°F (28°C to 34°C). Let ferment for 24 to 36 hours. Turn bags over after 12 hours. After 12 to 16 hours, white spots will appear; this is mycelium starting to grow.

8. Tempeh is ready when it forms solid blocks and beans are covered in thick white mycelium. If black spots appear around the aeration holes, it is not a problem, just a sign that it is ready.

9. Refrigerate or freeze immediately to prevent overfermentation. Tempeh produces heat as it ferments, so be careful not to pile the bags on top of one another. If you do, the middle of the pile risks overfermenting. Overfermented tempeh can develop a rancid odor and many black spots, not to mention intimidating its neighbors in the fridge.

Tempeh is always eaten cooked. It is cut into cubes or slices and often marinated, then grilled in a skillet, roasted in the oven or barbecued on skewers. Or it is made into Veggie Burgers (page 177).

Keeps in the refrigerator for up to 48 hours or in the freezer for 6 months.

TIP

If you use a dehydrator as an incubator, place bags on a perforated foil sheet to prevent tempeh from drying out.

Tempeh is one of those special fermentations that take most Westerners out of their eating comfort zone. A common food in Indonesia, where it is often produced in an artisanal fashion, it's a little like "Indonesian Brie," with its round disk shape and coating of mycelium (the name of the fur that produces the mold). Unlike Brie, however, tempeh is very easy to make. So while you're waiting 30 days for your sauerkraut to be ready, why not try making tempeh? It only takes 36 hours. In fermentation terms, that's equivalent to instant gratification!

LEVEL OF DIFFICULTY

🏺 🏺 🏺

TYPE OF FERMENTATION
Lactic

PREPARATION TIME
1 hour + 30 minutes cooking time

FERMENTATION TIME
14 days

EQUIPMENT
Bowls, large pot, saucepan, 2-quart (2 L) glass jar, airlock (ideally), dehydrator or oven, baking sheet (optional)

SEITAN

2²/₃ cups (360 g) all-purpose flour or 2 cups (240 g) vital wheat gluten (approx.)

½ tsp (2 g) salt

Water

MARINADE

¾ cup (135 g) cane sugar

2 tbsp (30 mL) paprika

1 tbsp (15 mL) grated gingerroot

1 tbsp (15 g) salt

1 tsp (5 mL) freshly ground black pepper

½ tsp (2 mL) grated or ground turmeric

¼ cup (60 mL) water

3 tbsp (45 mL) honey

3 tbsp (45 mL) Shoyu (page 151), tamari or Miso (page 148)

2 tsp (10 mL) vegetable oil

1 tbsp (15 mL) plain yogurt (page 107) or ¼ cup (60 mL) sauerkraut juice (page 41)

fermented SEITAN Jerky

1. *Seitan:* In a large bowl, using a fork, mix flour, salt and 1½ cups (375 mL) water until dough is firm and no longer sticks to the fork. Add flour or water as needed.

2. Using your hands, knead dough (as you would for bread) for 5 minutes, then form a ball.

3. If using all-purpose flour, under a stream of cold running tap water, knead dough in bowl for 15 minutes or until water turns clear. The ball of dough should have diminished in size. If using gluten flour, skip this step.

4. In a large pot, bring 8 cups (2 L) water to a boil over high heat. Cut dough ball into 4 pieces and place in water. Cook over low heat for 30 minutes. Drain. You now have seitan. This can substitute for chicken in any recipe, especially if you want to avoid killing a chicken (or if you are trying to assassinate someone who is allergic to gluten).

5. Cut seitan into ¼-inch (0.5 cm) thick slices. Set aside in a bowl.

6. *Marinade:* In a saucepan, combine sugar, paprika, ginger, salt, pepper, turmeric, water, honey, shoyu and oil; heat over medium heat, stirring until sugar is dissolved. Let cool at room temperature (under 86°F/30°C). Stir in yogurt.

7. Pour marinade over seitan and stir gently to avoid tearing seitan.

8. Transfer seitan with marinade to the jar. Close jar and set airlock (or slightly unscrew lid to allow carbon dioxide from the fermentation to escape). Let ferment out of direct light at room temperature for 14 days.

9. Drain seitan. Lay slices on racks in a single layer in a dehydrator or on a baking sheet; discard excess liquid. Dehydrate for 12 hours at 104°F (40°C) or bake for 3 hours in oven at the lowest temperature. Jerky should be almost completely dry, but still flexible.

To bring along on a hike and to keep handy in the glove compartment for those times when you find yourself stuck in traffic and craving a snack.

Keeps in an airtight container at room temperature for 6 months.

TYPES OF FERMENTATION
Mold, amylolytic

PREPARATION TIME
4 hours + 12 hours soaking time

FERMENTATION TIME
36 to 48 hours

EQUIPMENT
Scale, 1¼-gallon (5 L) plastic bucket, electric steam cooker or steamer basket, cotton cloths, bowl, small fine-mesh sieve or tea ball, airtight glass or plastic containers, incubator, digital kitchen thermometer, dehydrator (optional)

RICE Koji

FOR 4 LBS 6 OZ (2 KG)

2 lbs 3 oz (1 kg) high-quality Japanese short-grain white rice

Water

Dried beans or peas (for example, soybeans or chickpeas) for steamer

2 or 3 pinches koji culture (*Aspergillus oryzae*; see Where To Buy This Strange Stuff, page 197)

1 tsp (5 mL) cornstarch

1. Rinse rice under cold running water until water runs clear. Drain.

2. In the bucket, soak rice in 20 cups (5 L) water at room temperature for 12 hours.

3. Place a layer of dried beans or peas in bottom of steam cooker or steamer basket (rice should never be submerged in water for cooking) and cover with a cloth. This layer will protect rice from excess moisture from the steam. Without this layer, the rice will become too moist and the fermentation that follows will encourage the development of undesirable bacteria instead of mold. Attention: carefully place cloth between beans and rice, as you will need to separate them.

4. Place rice on cloth, spread rice flat and fold cloth over rice. Steam for 1 hour or until rice loses its opacity, turns shiny and is rubbery in texture. If the entire grain is slightly translucent, that means it's cooked!

5. Wash your hands carefully. Transfer rice to a clean bowl. Using your hands, break up lumps to separate grains. Let cool to 95°F (35°C), mixing frequently with your hands to help it cool.

6. Mix koji culture with cornstarch. Using a fine-mesh sieve, sprinkle cornstarch mixture over entire surface of rice and mix well (always using clean hands, as dictated by tradition) to distribute the spores.

If you don't have the courage to tackle this recipe (which we agree is fairly complicated), there's nothing to prevent you from making the koji-based fermentations in this book. You can buy koji fresh, frozen or dried (see Where to Buy This Strange Stuff, page 197). Once you feel braver, you can always come back to this recipe.

7. Line bottom of an airtight container with clean cotton cloth and spread rice on top. Cover with another cloth and put lid on without sealing airtight.

8. Place container in an incubator (the oven of an electric range, with heat off but oven light on, or a cooler containing jars of hot water, or another device of your creation) at 82°F to 93°F (28°C to 34°C).

9. Check temperature, ideally with a digital thermometer inserted directly in rice (to ensure it measures the temperature of the rice and not the air in the incubator). Adjust temperature if needed. If incubator is not sufficiently warm or fluctuates too much, add jars of very hot water to raise the ambient temperature.

10. Every 8 to 12 hours, remove rice. Check that the grains are not too dry (hard) or wet (shiny) and are still rubbery in texture. Mix rice well with your hands, taking care to break up lumps. If the grains are too dry and have hardened, spray a little water on them and mix well.

11. After 12 to 16 hours in the incubator, little spots of fuzzy white mold should start to form on grains of rice.

12. After 30 to 36 hours in the incubator, rice should be covered in a thin layer of white mold and give off a scent that is somewhere between mozzarella and vanilla with a hint of dirty socks! If the odor of socks is very pronounced and rice is wet, it's better to start over. If there is no growth after 36 hours, it's possible the rice is too dry. Spray again with water and wrap it all in a plastic bag to retain moisture.

Continued on page 140

13. After 36 to 48 hours in the incubator, rice will be almost entirely covered in white filaments. When the slightest tinge of green or yellow appears on the odd grain of rice, the koji is ready. Attention: if the rice turns completely dark green, it means the koji has made spores and cannot be used for sake, but can be used for shoyu.

14. Spread rice in a thin layer in an airtight container and refrigerate. Koji produces heat as it ferments, which is why it needs to be spread in a layer thinner than 1¼ inch (3 cm) to halt the fermentation quickly and evenly.

15. If desired, you can dry the koji in a dehydrator, at a temperature no higher than 113°F (45°C), to preserve the enzymes you will want to use in future fermentations (see pages 143 to 149).

You deserve a big pat on the back: you've just made the most complicated recipe in the book. And now you have enough koji to make 5 years' worth of miso!

Keeps in an airtight container in the refrigerator for up to 4 weeks or in the freezer for up to 1 year.

TIP

Another possibility for your incubator is to use a thermocirculator (also known as a sous vide immersion circulator) in a bucket of water placed inside your dishwasher — the humid environment this creates is basically Valhalla for mold.

Aspergillus oryzae is the filamentous mold in koji. If you find this repugnant, remember that many Westerners regularly consume it without knowing. Shoyu (soy sauce), miso, sake and tamari are foods that would not exist without this master of sugar decomposition. This recipe does not produce a fermentation to be consumed as is. Although it is edible, koji is primarily the basic ingredient in the other fermentations of Asian origin you will find in this book. Koji is the Japanese equivalent of the malted barley of Western countries, but with many more culinary uses!

VARIATION

Soy and Wheat Koji
for Shoyu

REPLACE RICE WITH:

2 lbs 3 oz (1 kg) cracked wheat or bulgur wheat

2 lbs 3 oz (1 kg) dried soybeans

REPLACE STEPS 1 TO 4 ON PAGE 138 WITH THESE STEPS:

1. Preheat broiler. Spread wheat on a baking sheet and broil for 1 to 2 minutes to toast grains. Be careful not to burn them!

2. In a bowl, combine soybeans and toasted wheat, cover with water and soak overnight. Drain.

3. Place a layer of dried beans or peas in bottom of steam cooker or steamer basket (the soy and wheat mixture for fermenting should never be submerged in water for cooking) and cover with a cloth. This layer will protect the soy and wheat mixture from excess moisture from the steam. Without this layer, the soy and wheat mixture will become too moist and the fermentation that follows will encourage the growth of undesirable bacteria instead of mold. Attention: carefully place cloth between beans and the soy/wheat mixture, so they can be separated.

4. Place soy and wheat mixture on cloth, spread flat and fold cloth over top. Steam for 90 minutes. Continue with step 5 of the Rice Koji recipe, taking the same precautions for controlling moisture and temperature. The appearance of green spores on the grains is desirable in this case.

Once it is thoroughly covered in mold, the soy and wheat koji is ready for making Shoyu (page 151).

Keeps in an airtight container in the refrigerator for 1 week or in the freezer for 1 year.

LEVEL OF DIFFICULTY

TYPES OF FERMENTATION
Mold, amylolytic, alcoholic (10% to 12%), lactic

PREPARATION TIME
2 hours + 1 night soaking

FERMENTATION TIME
8 to 12 days

EQUIPMENT
Scale, bowl, electric steam cooker or steamer basket, cotton cloths, spray bottle with sanitizing solution (see page 23) or vodka, 1-gallon (4 L) carboy or bucket with lid, airlock, airtight glass bottles, cotton brewing bag

Sake
(JAPANESE RICE WINE)

FOR 12 CUPS (3 L)

2 cups (400 g) short-grain white rice

Filtered water

Dried beans (for example, soybeans or chickpeas) for steamer

1 packet (5 g) sake or champagne yeast or dry bread yeast

18 oz (500 g) fresh or frozen Rice Koji (page 138) or 9 oz (250 g) dried rice koji

1 tbsp (15 mL) cane sugar

¼ cup (60 mL) freshly squeezed lemon juice (approx.)

Rice syrup (optional)

1. Rinse half the rice (1 cup/200 g) under cold running water until water runs clear. Drain. Place rinsed rice in a bowl, add water to cover and soak overnight.

2. Place a layer of dried beans or peas in bottom of steam cooker or steamer basket (rice should never be submerged in water for cooking) and cover with a cloth. This layer will protect rice from excess moisture from the steam. Without this layer, the rice will become too moist and the fermentation that follows will encourage the development of undesirable bacteria instead of mold. Attention: carefully place cloth between beans and rice, as you will need to separate them.

3. Place rice on cloth, spread rice flat and fold cloth over rice. Steam for 1 hour or until rice loses its opacity, turns shiny and is rubbery in texture. If the entire grain is slightly translucent, that means it's cooked!

4. Spread rice on a dry cloth and let cool to 77°F (25°C).

5. Disinfect equipment by spraying with sanitizing solution and wiping with clean cloths.

6. In carboy, mix yeast, rice koji, sugar, 4 cups (1 L) filtered water and lemon juice. Let stand for 15 minutes. Add cooled rice and mix well with a sanitized large spoon.

7. Close carboy with an airtight lid equipped with an airlock and let ferment out of direct light at 60°F to 72°F (16°C to 22°C) for 5 days. Shake vigorously to mix at 24-hour intervals.

8. On Day 5, rinse, soak, then cook the remaining rice according to steps 1 to 4.

Continued on page 144

Sake ... CONTINUED

9. Add cooled rice to carboy and mix well with a sanitized large spoon or by shaking carboy. Close carboy with the lid and airlock (or just loosely cover carboy with the lid) and continue fermentation at a lower temperature (54°F to 61°F/12°C to 16°C). For the first 3 days, shake vigorously to mix at 24-hour intervals. Let ferment until there are hardly any bubbles left and/or mixture separates into a transparent liquid on top and white sediment on the bottom. This can take more than 1 week.

10. Place carboy in refrigerator (or outdoors if temperature is between 23°F and 41°F (−5°C and 5°C) for a few days to help liquid settle.

11. Carefully transfer clear liquid to bottles. This is clear sake. Pour the white liquid from the bottom of the carboy through a cotton brewing bag, pressing gently to release liquid without allowing too many solids to pass through. This sake is called nigori, which means "cloudy." Bottle immediately and refrigerate. Tip from a pro: dehydrate the solids and reduce them to powder to use as a soup base.

12. If the flavor of either sake is a little bland, add lemon juice or rice syrup to taste (yes, sake is both sweet and acidic).

Sake can be enjoyed hot or cold, according to your preference. In our humble opinion, it is better hot, in a Thermos, while sitting around a campfire in winter.

Keeps for 1 month in the refrigerator. To keep sake for 6 months without refrigeration, pasteurize it: in a large pot, bring sake to a boil; remove from heat and bottle while hot (more than 158°F/70°C).

TIP

To produce makgeolli, the Korean cousin of sake, replace the rice koji with 3¹⁄₂ oz (100 g) nuruk (dried Korean wild rice koji), which can be found at Korean supermarkets.

Sake, the Japanese spirit of mythical status, is produced according to the strictest traditional standards. During the rice harvest in fall, brewers in the sake factories work day and night preparing koji. A short distance away, workers in a circle rinse pouches of rice with the diligence and coordination of a troupe of professional dancers. It is impossible to get a glimpse inside the koji room. No one is permitted to enter. Sake producers try to distinguish themselves: who will demonstrate the deepest respect for artisan brewing regulations and maintain the highest standards of freshness for water and rice. The best sake is the result of the most concerted effort. Since you probably don't have an entire season to dedicate to making sake, and after two days' absence from work your colleagues will start absconding with your office supplies, we suggest a shortened version of the sake recipe, which will still yield a fine product. As you experiment, you can gradually explore the more complex methods of production, which will keep you busy during your retirement.

We are completely under amazake's spell — for its wonderful, comforting flavor and because it's such a good example of the magic of fermentation. The koji digests the starch and complex carbohydrates in the rice and transforms them into simple sugars. Starch is not sweet, but simple sugars like maltose and glucose are. Thus, bland rice soup, when you add koji and then ferment it, turns very sweet in just one day.

TYPES OF FERMENTATION
Mold, amylolytic, lactic

PREPARATION TIME
1 hour

FERMENTATION TIME
24 hours

EQUIPMENT
**Scale, 16-cup (4 L) pot, blender
or food processor, incubator,
airtight glass bottles**

Amazake

FOR 16 CUPS (4 L)

1²⁄₃ cups (300 g) short-grain white rice

Pinch salt

Water

1 tbsp (15 mL) freshly squeezed lemon juice

6¹⁄₂ oz (185 g) fresh or frozen Rice Koji (page 138) or 3 oz (90 g) dried rice koji

1 vanilla bean, split

1 cup (250 mL) unsweetened almond milk

1 tsp (5 mL) ground cinnamon

1. Rinse rice under cold running water until water runs clear.

2. In a large pot, combine rice, salt, 8 cups (2 L) water and lemon juice. Cook over medium heat for 30 minutes to make a "rice soup": overcooked rice in too much water.

3. Add 4 cups (1 L) cold water to help mixture cool down to under 108°F (42°C). Add koji.

4. In blender or food processor, purée mixture until consistency is almost uniform.

5. Pour mixture into a shallow container (without a cover), place in an incubator (a dehydrator or the oven of an electric range, with heat off but oven light on) and maintain temperature between 86°F and 104°F (30°C and 40°C) for 24 hours.

6. Taste mixture; it should be very sweet. Add vanilla, almond milk and cinnamon.

7. Transfer mixture to a clean pot and heat over medium-high heat, stirring constantly to prevent it from sticking to the bottom. Bring to a boil, then remove from heat. This will pasteurize the amazake and prevent it from turning very bitter after 1 or 2 days.

8. Adjust with water to reduce sweetness or add more spices to taste. Discard vanilla bean.

9. Pour into bottles while still hot, quickly seal airtight, then refrigerate.

Drink as is, hot or cold, for a quick breakfast, or add a few drops of rum for a comforting dessert.

Keeps in the refrigerator for up to 2 months. Once opened, keep refrigerated and consume within 5 days.

LEVEL OF DIFFICULTY

TYPES OF FERMENTATION
Lactic, proteolytic, amylolytic

PREPARATION TIME
2 hours + 8 to 12 hours soaking

FERMENTATION TIME
2 to 8 months(!)

EQUIPMENT
Scale, bowls, 16-cup (4 L) pot, blender or food processor or ricer, 1-gallon (4 L) bucket with lid, plastic wrap, small plate (as a weight), airlock

2 lbs 3 oz (1 kg) dried soybeans

Spring water

18 oz (500 g) fresh Rice Koji (page 138), or 10½ oz (300 g) dried koji and 1⅓ cups + 1 tbsp (340 mL) water

1⅔ cups (400 g) fine sea salt + some for sprinkling

1 tbsp (15 mL) unpasteurized miso

1. Rinse soybeans in plenty of water. Place in a bowl and cover with water. Let soak overnight (for 8 to 12 hours). Drain and, if desired, remove skins.

2. Place beans in a large pot and add spring water to cover (at least 8 cups/2 L). Cook over medium-low heat for 2 hours. Drain and set aside 4 cups (1 L) cooking water. Let beans cool to room temperature.

3. In a large bowl, combine koji (or dried koji and water), salt and miso.

4. In blender or food processor, or using a ricer, purée soybeans.

5. Add purée to koji mixture. Using your hands (it's easier and more enjoyable), mix ingredients well to incorporate ferments. Texture should resemble modeling dough. Add a little cooking water if needed to obtain a smooth but firm paste.

6. Transfer paste to the bucket, one handful at a time, throwing it (yes, throwing it!) at the bottom of the bucket. This will help prevent bubbles from forming. It also lowers stress levels. Level out the surface, sprinkle with a few pinches of salt and cover with plastic wrap directly on the surface to prevent miso from drying out or turning moldy. Place a small plate on top as a weight.

7. Close with lid equipped with an airlock and let ferment at room temperature for 6 to 8 months. It can be eaten after 2 months, but it will be at its best after 8 months or more.

A marvelous seasoning for Warrior's Miso Soup (page 165), miso is also a nice substitute for broth in any recipe and for salt in sauces and marinades. A small spoonful a day of miso in cold water is a good source of probiotics. You can also do like the Japanese and have a bowl of light miso soup to start the day off right.

Keeps for 5 years in the refrigerator. If desired, you can store it in smaller containers, such as mason jars.

Miso paste and soy sauce are used in the same way, the only difference being that miso is solid and soy sauce is liquid. Miso has a delicate perfume, aromas that are richer and more complex than shoyu, and a flavor reminiscent of Australian Vegemite or British Marmite. With a little butter on toast, miso is pure umami. Miso fermentation is one of the longest fermentations in this book, but making it is surprisingly simple.

Unlike miso, which is made from rice koji, shoyu is made from soy and wheat koji. Like miso, shoyu is a long fermentation. Raw soy sauce has a much more pronounced flavor than the industrial soy sauces we are used to. The finished product can be diluted with water or sweetened with maple syrup until it pleases your palate.

TYPES OF FERMENTATION
Lactic, proteolytic, amylolytic

PREPARATION TIME
2 hours

FERMENTATION TIME
4 to 8 months

EQUIPMENT
Scale, bowl, 2½-gallon (10 L) bucket with lid, plastic wrap (optional), airlock, cotton brewing bag or cheesecloth, two 1¼-gallon (5 L) buckets, bottles

FOR 32 CUPS (8 L)

1 tbsp (15 mL) homemade Miso (page 148) or store-bought unpasteurized miso

Filtered water

2 cups (500 g) salt

3 lbs (1.5 kg) fresh or frozen Soy and Wheat Koji for Shoyu (page 142)

Granulated sugar, pure maple syrup or vinegar to taste (optional)

Shoyu
(SOY SAUCE)

1. In a bowl, using a fork, mix miso with ¼ cup (60 mL) water. Mixture should be as smooth and consistent as possible.

2. In a 2½-gallon (10 L) bucket, combine 11¼ cups (2.3 L) water, salt, koji and miso mixture. If desired, cover surface with plastic wrap directly on the surface to prevent mixture from drying out or turning moldy.

3. Close with lid equipped with an airlock and let ferment at room temperature for 4 to 8 months.

4. Open and sniff! At the end of the fermentation process, the "fruity" aromas should be quite pronounced. If a little white or blue-green mold is visible, remove this top layer with a spoon. If forest green mold has grown, unfortunately you will have to discard the entire batch and start over.

5. Transfer aromatic paste to a cotton brewing bag or cheesecloth to strain it, pressing firmly with your hands to release as much liquid as possible. (Set aside solids and dry in a dehydrator to use later as a broth base.)

6. Transfer liquid to a 1¼-gallon (5 L) bucket and continue fermentation in the same way for 3 to 5 days, to let it settle.

7. Carefully pour liquid into another 1¼-gallon (5 L) bucket to separate liquid from sediment. At this stage, it is possible to adjust the flavor of the shoyu with sugar, maple syrup or vinegar, while preserving a product that is salty enough to have a long shelf life.

8. Transfer liquid to bottles and refrigerate (see tip).

As we all know, soy sauce is best poured generously over vanilla ice cream...

Keeps for 2 years in the refrigerator.

TIP

To stabilize the flavor and keep at room temperature for 5 years, fill bottles, seal airtight and boil for 30 minutes.

on the
menu

From FEASTS to Snacks

NOW THAT YOU HOLD ALL THE SECRETS to preparing these lively and effervescent concoctions, you still need some idea of how to make them part of your diet. Scarfing down a jar of fermented garlic scapes with a fork may be fun, but we don't recommend it in public on a daily basis. On the other hand, as an accompaniment to a meal or for adding zest to a sauce without using up an entire saltshaker, your garlic scapes will have a place in your heart forever.

We all have fridges filled with jars. Some jars may be opened only once a month, but oh, the treats that lie within! Your fermentations will turn your quick lunch on the go into a memorable meal break. They spice up a corner of the dish, add a dash of "wow!" to a simple sandwich and even brighten up a boring gin and tonic.

LEVEL OF DIFFICULTY

PREPARATION TIME
45 minutes

EQUIPMENT
Skillet, blender, two 1-pint (500 mL) jars or classic ketchup bottles (empty and clean)

Ketchup

FOR 2 CUPS (500 ML)

1 tbsp (15 mL) olive oil

2 cloves garlic, minced

1 small yellow onion, chopped

1 stalk celery, chopped

1 tomato, diced and drained

¼ bulb fennel, chopped

1 tsp (5 mL) sweet or smoked paprika

1 tsp (5 mL) salt

½ tsp (2 mL) freshly ground black pepper

¼ tsp (1 mL) ground cloves

1 cup (250 mL) tomato paste

½ cup (125 mL) Apple Cider Vinegar (page 99)

¼ cup (60 mL) water

¼ cup (60 mL) pure maple syrup

1. In a skillet, heat oil over medium heat. Sauté garlic, onion, celery, tomato, fennel, paprika, salt, pepper and cloves for 10 to 15 minutes or until vegetables are softened.

2. Stir in tomato paste, vinegar, water and maple syrup. Boil, uncovered, for 15 minutes or until reduced and thickened. Remove from heat and let cool for 10 minutes.

3. In blender, purée mixture into a smooth paste. Taste and adjust salt, vinegar, water and maple syrup to your preference. Blend to combine.

4. Pour into jars or ketchup bottles and cover with lids.

To carry in your bag every day in case you stumble over some french fries.

Keeps for 4 months in the refrigerator.

PREPARATION TIME
20 minutes

EQUIPMENT
Rimmed baking sheet or skillet, food processor

Fermented Garlic Scape and BRAZIL NUT Bruschetta Tapenade

FOR 2¼ CUPS (550 ML)

¼ cup (25 g) sun-dried tomatoes

¼ cup (35 g) pumpkin seeds

Pinch sea salt

1 cup (220 g) drained Muscovite Garlic Scapes (page 63)

½ cup (35 g) Brazil nuts

2 tbsp (8 g) nutritional yeast

Pinch hot pepper flakes

¼ cup (60 mL) olive oil

1 tbsp (15 mL) Shoyu (page 151) or tamari

1. Place sun-dried tomatoes in a bowl, cover with water and let soak for 10 minutes. Drain.

2. Preheat broiler, if using. To broil, spread pumpkin seeds on a rimmed baking sheet and season with sea salt; broil to toast lightly. (Or lightly toast in skillet over medium heat, stirring constantly.) Immediately transfer to a bowl and let cool.

3. In food processor, combine sun-dried tomatoes, garlic scapes, Brazil nuts, nutritional yeast, hot pepper flakes, oil and shoyu; process into a uniform paste. Add pumpkin seeds, then grind for just a few seconds, making sure to preserve crunchy pieces.

Spread on slices of hot toasted baguette, sprinkle with shavings of Parmesan cheese and devour.

Keeps for 2 weeks in an airtight container in the refrigerator.

LEVEL OF DIFFICULTY

PREPARATION TIME
10 minutes for spread;
3 minutes for vinaigrette

EQUIPMENT
Spread: Skillet, toaster

Vinaigrette: Airtight jar

Black Garlic, TWO WAYS: spread and VINAIGRETTE

BLACK GARLIC SPREAD ON TOAST WITH AVOCADO

2 tbsp (18 g) sesame seeds

½ tsp (2 mL) sea salt

1 tbsp (15 mL) coconut oil

½ cup (25 g) dried seaweed flakes (dulse)

1 large slice Country-Style Miche (page 125)

3 cloves Black Garlic (page 64), skin removed, mashed with a fork

1 avocado, cut into thin strips

1 handful salad greens or microsprouts (such as arugula, watercress or alfalfa)

BLACK GARLIC VINAIGRETTE

1 bulb Black Garlic (page 64)

Pinch sea salt

½ cup (125 mL) olive oil

2 tbsp (30 mL) Shoyu (page 151)

1 tbsp (15 mL) pure maple syrup

1 tbsp (15 mL) balsamic vinegar

BLACK GARLIC SPREAD ON TOAST WITH AVOCADO

1. In a skillet over medium heat, toast sesame seeds with sea salt, stirring constantly. Set aside in a small bowl.

2. In the same skillet, melt coconut oil over low heat. Toast seaweed flakes until their color changes and they are crispy. Set aside.

3. Toast bread. Spread a thin layer of mashed black garlic on toasted bread and top with strips of avocado. Garnish with greens, toasted sesame seeds and crispy seaweed.

Take a bite and smile with contentment.

BLACK GARLIC VINAIGRETTE

1. Remove skin from garlic cloves and mash cloves with a fork in a bowl.

2. In a jar, combine mashed garlic, salt, oil, shoyu, maple syrup and vinegar. Close lid and shake vigorously, like a paint shaker machine. Makes about ¾ cup (175 mL).

Pour over slices of multicolored tomatoes. If a craving for protein is making you feel like a flexitarian, pour it over a slice of toasted Country-Style Miche topped with scrambled egg, or over a bagel with smoked salmon.

Vinaigrette keeps for 1 week in the refrigerator.

No one knows where the "dragon" comes from, but every vegan restaurant can attest to the popularity of this dish!

Dragon Bowl

AND ITS DIVINE SAUCES

LEVEL OF DIFFICULTY

PREPARATION TIME
10 minutes (+ 30 to 60 minutes soaking time)

EQUIPMENT
Blender (optional), airtight glass jar(s), skillet

DRAGON SAUCE

- ⅔ cup (85 g) cashews
- 1 clove garlic
- ⅔ cup (40 g) nutritional yeast
- 1 tsp (5 mL) sea salt
- Pinch cayenne pepper
- 1 cup (250 mL) olive oil
- ¼ cup (60 mL) filtered water
- 3 tbsp (45 mL) Shoyu (page 151) or tamari
- 2 tbsp (30 mL) pure maple syrup
- 1 tsp (5 mL) Apple Cider Vinegar (page 99)

MISO AND TAHINI SAUCE

- 1 tsp (5 mL) minced garlic
- ¼ cup (60 mL) Miso (page 148)
- ½ cup (125 mL) water
- ¼ cup (60 mL) sunflower oil
- 1 tbsp (15 mL) tahini
- 1 tbsp (15 mL) pure maple syrup
- 1 tbsp (15 mL) Apple Cider Vinegar
- 1 tsp (5 mL) tamari

DRAGON BOWL

- 1 block Tempeh (page 134), cut into strips
- 2 cups (325 g) hot cooked rice
- 18 oz (500 g) steamed mixed vegetables (see tip)
- 1 large handful sunflower shoots (see tip)

DRAGON SAUCE

1. In a bowl, soak cashews in enough water to cover for 30 to 60 minutes. Drain cashews.

2. In a blender, combine soaked cashews, garlic, nutritional yeast, salt, cayenne, oil, water, shoyu, maple syrup and vinegar; purée into a uniform sauce. Pour into a glass jar.

To eat with a spoon without your roommate noticing or to add generously to a Dragon Bowl.

Keeps for 1 week in the refrigerator.

MISO AND TAHINI SAUCE

1. In a glass jar, combine garlic, miso, water, oil, tahini, maple syrup, vinegar and tamari; close lid and shake vigorously.

To use as a sauce on anything or as a substitute for Dragon Sauce in a Dragon Bowl.

Keeps for 1 week in the refrigerator.

DRAGON BOWL

1. In a skillet, in batches, sauté tempeh strips for 3 minutes on each side.

2. Place rice and steamed vegetables in a bowl. Add toasted tempeh and sunflower shoots.

3. Pour Dragon Sauce or Miso and Tahini Sauce liberally on top and mix together.

TIP

For the steamed vegetables, try a mixture of bok choy, bell pepper, zucchini, eggplant and/or carrot. In place of the sunflower shoots, try green pea shoots or salad greens such as arugula or mâche.

Grape Leaves
WITH SORGHUM,
honey and
TOASTED ALMONDS

FOR 12 ROLLS

1 cup (200 g) sorghum

3 cups (750 mL) water

½ cup (75 g) almonds

20 fresh mint leaves, chopped

½ bunch fresh parsley, chopped

1 tsp (5 mL) sea salt

Pinch freshly ground black pepper

Juice of ½ lemon

1 tbsp (15 mL) liquid honey

1 tbsp (15 mL) Shoyu (page 151) or tamari

1 tbsp (15 mL) olive oil

12 Lactofermented Grape Leaves (page 54)

1. Rinse sorghum in plenty of water, then drain.

2. In a skillet, over medium heat, toast sorghum, stirring constantly, for 5 minutes or until lightly browned.

3. In a saucepan, combine toasted sorghum and water; bring to a boil over medium-high heat. Reduce heat to low, cover and simmer for 40 minutes. Drain, let cool and set aside.

4. Preheat broiler. Spread almonds on a rimmed baking sheet. Broil to toast almonds. Transfer to a bowl and let cool, then chop.

5. In a bowl, mix sorghum, almonds, mint, parsley, salt, pepper, lemon juice, honey, shoyu and oil.

6. Spread grape leaves on a cutting board. Place 1 heaping tbsp (15 mL) sorghum mixture in the center of each leaf. Roll up leaves as you like. Even if they aren't as pretty as in the photo, it's what's inside that counts!

To eat cold or to keep up to 2 days in an airtight container in the refrigerator.

This recipe makes more filling than you need to fill the grape leaves. Eat it while pondering the choices you've made in life.

LEVEL OF DIFFICULTY

PREPARATION TIME
15 minutes

EQUIPMENT
Saucepan

FOR 4 SERVINGS

1 tbsp (15 mL) sesame oil

½ red onion, slivered

1 cup (100 g) wild or domestic mushrooms

4 cups (1 L) water

2 bok choy, chopped

2 sheets nori, cut into thin strips

¼ cup (12 g) dried wakame seaweed

2 tbsp (30 mL) grated gingerroot

¼ tsp (1 mL) cayenne pepper

Juice of ½ lime

Generous 4 tbsp (60 mL) Miso (page 148)

A few sprigs fresh cilantro or a few shiso leaves for garnish

WARRIOR'S Miso Soup

1. In a saucepan, heat oil over medium heat. Sauté onion and mushrooms for 5 minutes.

2. Add water and increase heat to high. When water is about to boil, reduce heat to low and add bok choy, nori, wakame, ginger, cayenne and lime juice; simmer for 4 minutes. Remove from heat.

3. Remove 1 cup (250 mL) broth from the pan to a bowl and mix with miso, whisking until miso is completely melted. Pour concentrated miso into saucepan and stir.

4. Pour into small bowls and garnish with fresh cilantro or shiso leaves. Eat with an Asian soup spoon, because it tastes best that way.

After a hard day's labor, this soup is a well-deserved reward for the warrior in you.

Keeps for 2 days in an airtight container in the refrigerator.

PREPARATION TIME
10 minutes

EQUIPMENT
Glass jar, skillet

Wild Mushroom
SALAD with
kombucha vinaigrette

FOR 4 SERVINGS

KOMBUCHA VINAIGRETTE

¼ bunch fresh cilantro, chopped

1 tsp (5 mL) grated gingerroot

Pinch salt

⅓ cup + 2 tsp (85 mL) olive oil

¼ cup (60 mL) Kombucha Vinegar (page 89)

Generous 2 tbsp (30 mL) almond butter

1 tbsp (15 mL) liquid honey

1 tbsp (15 mL) Shoyu (page 151) or tamari

Cold water for diluting to taste

WILD MUSHROOM SALAD

2 tbsp (30 mL) olive oil

2 cups (200 g) fresh or rehydrated wild mushrooms (such as oyster or shiitake)

1 tsp (5 mL) salt

1 large endive, cut into thin strips

½ bulb fennel, cut into thin strips

1 small Asian pear, cut into thin strips

KOMBUCHA VINAIGRETTE

1. In a glass jar, combine cilantro, ginger, salt, oil, kombucha vinegar, almond butter, honey and shoyu; close lid and shake vigorously before a mirror while contemplating your muscles. Add a little cold water until you achieve the desired consistency.

WILD MUSHROOM SALAD

1. In a skillet, heat oil over medium heat. Sauté mushrooms with salt for 8 minutes or until mushrooms are slightly browned. Let cool.

2. Place endive, fennel and Asian pear in a salad bowl. Add cooled mushrooms. Pour sweetened kombucha vinaigrette on top (to taste) and mix well. Serve immediately.

To be accompanied by a glass of kombucha and eaten before your famished roommate is drawn by the scent.

The vinaigrette keeps for 2 weeks in the refrigerator. Excellent with the Wild Mushroom Salad or on your favorite salad greens.

David invented this recipe during a road trip in New Zealand, when he was living in his truck. This memorable meal was put together with all that was left to eat in his survival kit...

Millet SALAD with Crispy Tempeh

LEVEL OF DIFFICULTY

PREPARATION TIME
35 minutes

EQUIPMENT
Glass jar, skillet

FOR 1 SERVING

CRISPY TEMPEH

11 tbsp (170 g) peanut, almond or other nut butter

½ cup (125 mL) water

2 tbsp (30 mL) Miso (page 148)

1 tsp (5 mL) ground cumin

2 tbsp (30 mL) olive oil

1 clove garlic, minced

3½ oz (100 g) Spanish onion (1 medium), thinly sliced

2 blocks Tempeh (page 134), cut into cubes

MILLET SALAD

½ cup (80 g) cooked millet

½ head broccoli, cut into florets, steamed

¼ cup (35 g) Lactofermented Root Vegetables (page 42)

1 large handful microsprouts and/or salad greens (your choice)

CRISPY TEMPEH

1. In a glass jar, combine nut butter, water, miso and cumin; close lid and shake vigorously until you have a thick, uniform sauce — or not, if you don't feel like it.

2. In a skillet, heat oil over medium heat. Sauté garlic and onion for 1 minute. Add tempeh and cook, stirring, for 5 minutes or until tempeh is crispy. Pour in nut sauce and stir over low heat until water evaporates and tempeh is crispy.

MILLET SALAD

1. In a bowl, combine millet, broccoli, root vegetables and microsprouts. Add tempeh while still hot.

To be cooked over a burner in a Westfalia by the beach.

LEVEL OF DIFFICULTY

PREPARATION TIME
35 minutes

EQUIPMENT
Blender (optional), cloth

MISOZUKE rolls
WITH
Oof! SAUCE

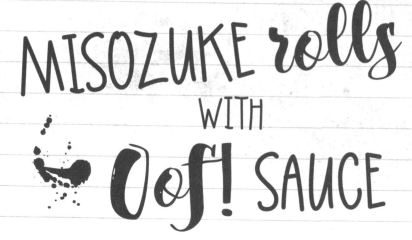

FOR 8 ROLLS

OOF! SAUCE

1 clove garlic, grated

3 tbsp (45 mL) peanut butter

2 tbsp (30 mL) Miso (page 148)

Juice of ½ lime

Pinch salt

Pinch cayenne pepper

¼ cup (60 mL) unsweetened almond milk (approx.)

ROLLS

8 medium-size rice papers

Warm water

A few Root Vegetables in Miso Brine (Misozuke or Tsukemono), julienned (page 45)

1 avocado, thinly sliced

1 handful fresh micro cilantro (or parsley, if you are put off by cilantro)

_____ (insert your creative idea here)

1 tsp (5 mL) black sesame seeds

16 lactofermented fiddleheads (page 53)

OOF! SAUCE

1. In a blender or in a bowl, combine garlic, peanut butter, miso, lime juice, salt and cayenne; purée or stir with a wooden spoon until blended. Add almond milk in a stream, through the hole in the lid with the motor running or while stirring, until desired texture is obtained.

ROLLS

1. Wet a clean cloth, wring out and spread over work surface.

2. Soak rice papers in warm water, one at a time, then lay them on damp cloth.

3. Top with julienned misozuke, avocado slices and micro cilantro. Add any other ingredient that inspires you! Sprinkle with sesame seeds.

4. Lay fiddleheads on top, then roll up very tightly. Eat cold, dipped in Oof! Sauce.

These rolls take any meal from blah to va va voom.

The sauce keeps in an airtight container in the refrigerator for 5 days.

Bibimbap

FOR 2 SERVINGS

1¼ cups (200 g) short-grain white rice

2 cups (500 mL) water

1 clove garlic, minced

1 tbsp (15 mL) cooking oil (your choice)

1 zucchini, thinly sliced

2 large eggs (optional)

1 bunch spinach leaves

2 tbsp (30 mL) toasted sesame oil

2 tbsp (30 mL) Shoyu (page 151) or tamari

1 cup (50 g) bean sprouts

1 red or orange bell pepper, cut into thin strips

1 cup (125 g) Classic Kimchi (page 49)

Bajan Hot Pepper Sauce (page 71) or Sriracha

¼ cup (40 g) toasted sesame seeds

1. Place rice and water in a rice cooker or steam cooker and cook according to package directions.

2. Meanwhile, in a skillet over low heat, sauté garlic in oil until fragrant. Add zucchini and sauté for 5 minutes. Remove from heat.

3. In a saucepan of boiling water, boil eggs in their shell for 2 minutes (see tip). Add spinach to water (to save time and water) and boil for 1 more minute.

4. Mix sesame oil and shoyu with cooked rice.

5. Place rice in middle of serving bowl, then place cooked zucchini mixture and spinach on one side, bean sprouts and bell pepper on other. Crack eggs on top, then add kimchi with its liquid and hot pepper sauce to taste. Garnish with sesame seeds.

Say "bibimbap" 10 times quickly without stammering. Once you've met the challenge, dig in with chopsticks and enjoy.

TIP

Instead of boiling the eggs, you can crack them raw into the salad and let the hot ingredients cook the egg. Either way, do cook the spinach in a saucepan of boiling water for 1 minute. (Caution: undercooked eggs carry a risk of salmonella, so this option should be avoided by pregnant women and anyone with a weakened immune system.)

LEVEL OF DIFFICULTY

PREPARATION TIME
15 minutes

EQUIPMENT
Skillet

FOR 4 SERVINGS

2 tsp (10 mL) olive oil

½ Spanish onion, finely chopped

2 blocks Tempeh (page 134), cut into cubes

2 small tomatoes, diced

1 large handful spinach

½ bunch fresh dill

3 tbsp (12 g) nutritional yeast

2 tbsp (30 mL) Shoyu (page 151) or tamari

½ tsp (2 mL) sea salt

¼ tsp (1 mL) cayenne pepper

TEMPEH "Omelet"

1. In a skillet, heat oil over low heat. Sauté onion for 4 minutes or until translucent.

2. Add tempeh cubes and cook for 5 minutes, stirring constantly.

3. Add tomatoes, spinach, dill, nutritional yeast, shoyu, salt and cayenne; simmer for 5 minutes, stirring frequently.

Serve in bed for Sunday or Monday brunch.

When the condiments, burgers and even the buns come out of your kitchen, it's something to be proud of! Substituting one or two store-bought ingredients for homemade, however, won't make you a cheater.

TEMPEH *Burger* WITH *Sauerkraut*

MARINATED TEMPEH

½ cup (125 mL) water

2 tbsp (30 mL) Apple Cider Vinegar (page 99)

3 tbsp (45 mL) Shoyu (page 151) or tamari

1 tbsp (15 mL) pure maple syrup

3 drops liquid smoke

1 tsp (5 mL) coriander seeds

1 slice Tempeh (page 134), in proportion to your appetite

FILLINGS

1 burger bun (see tip)

½ cup (70 g) Sauerkraut (page 41)

1 tbsp (15 mL) Mustard (page 67)

1 tbsp (15 mL) Ketchup (page 154)

1 large Pickled Cucumber (page 46), cut lengthwise into 4 slices

2 leaves lettuce

1 large handful sprouts (such as alfalfa, clover, mustard or daikon radish)

1 tomato, sliced

1. *Marinated Tempeh:* In a dish, combine water, vinegar, shoyu, maple syrup, liquid smoke and coriander seeds. Add tempeh, cover and marinate for at least 1 hour, or up to 8 hours if you have foresight.

2. In a skillet or on a barbecue grill, over medium heat, cook tempeh for 2 to 3 minutes on each side, or longer if you want it well-done.

3. *Fillings:* Fill bun with tempeh and your choice of condiments. For the rest, we don't need to draw you a picture.

Comfort food for an evening of solitary and nostalgic contemplation.

TIP

To make burger buns like you see in the photo, use the recipe for Country-Style Miche (page 125). Separate dough into 8 balls. Sprinkle with sesame seeds, if desired, and bake for 30 minutes, about half the time you would for the entire loaf of bread.

LEVEL OF DIFFICULTY

PREPARATION TIME
45 minutes

EQUIPMENT
Blender, barbecue grill (optional), baking sheet or sheet of foil

PURÉED EDAMAME

1 cup (140 g) shelled edamame

1 avocado

1/2 clove garlic

2 tbsp (30 mL) freshly squeezed lime juice

1/4 cup (60 mL) filtered water

Sea salt and freshly ground black pepper

ROASTED CAULIFLOWER

1 head cauliflower

2 tbsp (30 mL) olive oil

1 tbsp (15 mL) Shoyu (page 151) or tamari

MOLE

1/2 jalapeño pepper, seeds removed

1 tbsp (15 mL) unsweetened cocoa powder

1 tsp (5 mL) salt

2/3 cup (150 g) almond butter

1 tbsp (15 mL) Apple Cider Vinegar (page 99)

1 tbsp (15 mL) pure maple syrup

1/4 cup (60 mL) water (approx.)

TACOS

6 corn tortillas (ideally made by hand by a Mexican grandmother)

1 cup (125 g) Classic Kimchi (page 49)

ROASTED CAULIFLOWER
tacos WITH
kimchi
AND PURÉED EDAMAME

1. *Puréed Edamame:* In a blender, purée edamame with avocado, garlic, lime juice and water. Transfer to a bowl, season with salt and black pepper to taste and set aside.

2. *Roasted Cauliflower:* Preheat oven to 425°F (220°C) or heat barbecue grill to medium-high. Cut cauliflower into florets. Place on a baking sheet and sprinkle with oil and shoyu, or place on a sheet of foil folded up on the sides (but not sealed in a packet) and sprinkle with oil and shoyu. Bake for 30 minutes or grill for 20 minutes, until cauliflower is thoroughly cooked and slightly charred on the outside. Set aside and keep hot.

3. *Mole:* In clean blender, combine jalapeño, cocoa powder, salt, almond butter, vinegar and maple syrup; purée into a thick sauce, adding a little water if needed.

4. *Tacos:* Spread puréed edamame on tortillas, top with roasted cauliflower and kimchi and cover with mole.

To eat with your hands while drinking a michelada.

PREPARATION TIME
5 minutes + 5 minutes baking

EQUIPMENT
Barbecue grill (optional), baking sheet or slate baking stone

Pizza TRILOGY

All-purpose flour (for the baking sheet or stone)

POCAHONTAS

2 uncooked Naan (page 121)

3 tbsp (45 mL) chopped drained Muscovite Garlic Scapes (page 63)

1 cup (100 g) wild (edible!) mushrooms

1 handful arugula

Freshly grated Parmesan cheese, to taste

MARGHERITA

2 uncooked Naan (page 121)

¼ cup (60 mL) Homemade Cheese Spread (page 112)

¼ cup (25 g) chopped sun-dried tomatoes

1 fresh tomato, sliced the way you like

Green olives, pitted

Za'atar spices (page 111)

ALOHA

2 uncooked Naan (page 121)

4 slices fresh pineapple, cut into cubes

1 large handful Classic Kimchi (page 49)

8 pieces Fermented Seitan Jerky (page 137)

¼ cup (60 mL) Homemade Cheese Spread (page 112)

Sorrel

1. Preheat oven to 425°F (220°C) or preheat barbecue grill to medium-high. At the same time, heat baking sheet or baking stone.

2. Top uncooked naan with chosen ingredients.

3. Remove baking sheet or stone from oven or barbecue, sprinkle with flour and place pizzas on top.

4. Bake in oven or on covered barbecue for just the time it takes — not too little, not too long. Go on, we'll let you be the judge!

Ready in about 5 minutes. If in doubt, rely on the photo.

Because everyone knows the recipe for classic meringue made with egg whites, here's one made without eggs that's just as delicious!

PREPARATION TIME
50 minutes + soaking time

EQUIPMENT
Blender, 10-inch (25 cm) tart
pan with removable bottom,
saucepan, electric mixer

LEMON CONFIT
Meringue Pie

COCONUT, BRAZIL NUT AND POPPY SEED PIE CRUST

8 dried figs

Water

1 cup (120 g) Brazil nuts

3 cups (280 g) sweetened shredded coconut

2 tbsp (18 g) poppy seeds

1 tsp (5 mL) vanilla powder (or seeds scraped from ½ vanilla bean)

Grated zest of 1 lemon

Pinch sea salt

LEMON CONFIT CREAM

1 cup (192 g) cane sugar

1 cup (250 mL) freshly squeezed lemon juice (the juice of about 6 organic lemons)

½ cup (120 g) coconut butter

3 tbsp (45 mL) liquid sunflower lecithin

3 tbsp (50 g) finely chopped Lemon Confit (page 59)

VEGAN MERINGUE

½ cup (70 g) confectioners' (icing) sugar

6 tbsp + 2 tsp (100 mL) aquafaba (liquid from a 14-oz/398 mL can of chickpeas; see tip)

GARNISH (OPTIONAL)

Toasted coconut flakes

Zest left over from lemons used for Lemon Confit Cream

1. *Coconut, Brazil Nut and Poppy Seed Crust:* In a bowl, soak figs in water for 30 minutes.

2. In a blender, grind Brazil nuts and coconut to powder.

3. In a bowl, combine powdered nut mixture, poppy seeds, vanilla, lemon zest and salt.

4. Drain figs, setting aside some of the soaking water. In blender, grind figs to a paste, adding a little soaking water if needed.

5. Add fig paste to nut mixture. Mix until ball of pie dough is firm and malleable.

6. Using your hands, line bottom and sides of tart pan with dough. Set aside in freezer.

7. *Lemon Confit Cream:* In clean blender, combine sugar, lemon juice, coconut butter, lecithin and lemon confit; purée until texture is blended and uniform.

8. Spread lemon cream in pie crust. Refrigerate pie for about 30 minutes, until set.

9. *Vegan Meringue:* In a saucepan, combine sugar and aquafaba. Bring to a boil over high heat, stirring; reduce heat to low and simmer, stirring constantly, for 4 minutes.

10. Beat meringue with an electric mixer for 5 minutes (or whisk by hand for 30 minutes if you want to develop your forearm muscles).

11. When meringue forms soft peaks, spread gently on top of pie.

12. If desired, garnish with toasted coconut flakes and lemon zest. Or preheat broiler and broil pie for a few minutes to brown meringue.

To eat with your hands.

TIP

Another option for the aquafaba: If you are more of a purist and not the last-minute type, you can cook 1 cup (250 mL) dried chickpeas in 4 cups (1 L) water for 3 hours. Drain the chickpeas through a fine-mesh sieve set over a bowl to collect the cooking liquid. Save the chickpeas for another meal with friends.

PREPARATION TIME
20 minutes + 10 minutes baking

EQUIPMENT
12-cup muffin pan, saucepan

BLACK BEER
chocolate
lava cake

½ cup (114 g) coconut oil +
more for muffin pan

7 oz (200 g) dark chocolate,
chopped

4 large eggs

¾ cup (90 g) cane sugar

¼ cup (60 mL) black beer,
such as stout

½ cup (70 g) Kamut flour

Pinch sea salt

1. Preheat oven to 400°F (200°C). Grease muffin pan with coconut oil.

2. In a saucepan, over low heat, melt chocolate and ½ cup (114 g) coconut oil.

3. In a bowl, using a whisk, beat eggs, sugar and beer.

4. Add melted chocolate mixture and whisk.

5. Gradually add Kamut flour and whisk again.

6. Feel the excitement mounting.

7. Pour mixture into muffin pan, up to the rims.

8. Bake for 10 minutes (at the most!). Avoid overbaking — the centers should still be runny. Serve hot.

To be enjoyed with the rest of the black beer — you'll thank us.

There isn't much black beer in this recipe. And, as it happens, we haven't included a recipe for black beer in this book. But since all black beer is fermented and black beer is what makes this semi-baked recipe the best in the world...

KEFIR Milkshakes

LEVEL OF DIFFICULTY

PREPARATION TIME
10 minutes

EQUIPMENT
Blender

FOR 2 GLASSES PER VARIATION

STRAWBERRY FLIRT

2 cups (500 mL) Milk Kefir (page 108)

8 frozen strawberries

5 basil leaves

½ tsp (2 mL) vanilla powder (or seeds scraped from ½ vanilla bean)

Sweetener (optional)

SUN-KISSED

2 cups (500 mL) Milk Kefir (page 108)

2 frozen bananas, broken into chunks

3 or 4 hulled cardamom seeds

Pinch ground cinnamon

Pinch ground nutmeg

2 large ice cubes

Seeds scraped from 1 vanilla bean

Sweetener (optional)

1. In a blender, purée all ingredients. Add a little of your favorite sweetener if needed.

The Strawberry Flirt is to be shared on a Ferris wheel, while Sun-Kissed is to be shared in one glass with two straws.

LEVEL OF DIFFICULTY

PREPARATION TIME
10 minutes

EQUIPMENT
Blender

MONDAY
Cocktails

FOR 1 GLASS PER VARIATION

PINA COOLADA

1 pineapple (bottom third only)

1 cup (250 mL) Coconut Milk Kefir (page 108)

1 tsp (5 mL) vanilla powder

2 large ice cubes

VIRGIN MARY

1 large tomato (8 oz/250 g)

1 Pickled Cucumber (page 46)

1 red radish

½ red bell pepper

⅛ preserved lemon (see Lemon Confit, page 59)

Freshly ground black pepper

2 large ice cubes

½ celery stalk

PINA COOLADA

1. Cut off bottom third of pineapple. Cut out flesh and cut into pieces. Set aside the "shell."

2. In a blender, purée pineapple pieces, kefir, vanilla and ice cubes.

3. Pour mixture into shell, add two straws and enjoy.

VIRGIN MARY

1. In a blender, purée tomato (see tip), pickle, radish, bell pepper, lemon confit, black pepper to taste and ice cubes.

2. Pour into a glass, casually stir with celery stick and enjoy.

TIP

If the tomato isn't as juicy as you would have liked, add a little water.

LEVEL OF DIFFICULTY

PREPARATION TIME
5 minutes

EQUIPMENT
Cocktail shaker

SUNDAY Cocktails

FOR 1 GLASS PER VARIATION

DEEP BLUE

¼ cup (60 mL) Shrub Syrup (page 80)

1½ oz (45 mL) gin, preferably from Quebec

1 cup (250 mL) crushed ice

¾ cup (180 mL) Water Kefir (page 84)

HIPSTER'S DELIGHT

1 cup (250 mL) Ginger Beer (page 96)

1 oz (30 mL) whisky

Juice of ¼ lemon

1 tsp (5 mL) liquid honey

Ice cubes

½ slice lemon (optional)

DEEP BLUE

1. In a shaker, mix shrub and gin.

2. Place crushed ice in a glass. Pour gin mixture on top, then add kefir.

HIPSTER'S DELIGHT

1. In a shaker, mix ginger beer, whisky, lemon juice and honey.

2. Place a few ice cubes in a glass. Pour ginger beer mixture on top and garnish with ½ slice lemon, if desired.

Continued on page 192

LEVEL OF DIFFICULTY

PREPARATION TIME
5 minutes

EQUIPMENT
Cocktail shaker

SUNDAY Cocktails CONTINUED...

FOR 1 GLASS PER VARIATION

BEACH BUM

1 fresh jalapeño pepper, cut into thin slices, seeds removed

¼ cup (15 g) fresh cilantro leaves

1 cup (250 mL) carbonated water

1½ oz (45 mL) mezcal

1 tsp (5 mL) agave nectar

Juice of ¼ lime

2 large ice cubes

¼ cup (60 mL) Water Kefir (page 84)

YOUR SISTER ON A SKATEBOARD

½ cup (125 mL) apple juice

1½ oz (45 mL) dark rum

1 tsp (5 mL) Apple Cider Vinegar (page 99)

1 cinnamon stick

2 large ice cubes

½ cup (125 mL) homemade Kombucha (page 88)

BEACH BUM

1. In a shaker, mix jalapeño pepper, cilantro, water, mezcal, agave nectar and lime juice.

2. Place ice cubes in a glass. Pour mezcal mixture on top, then add kefir.

YOUR SISTER ON A SKATEBOARD

1. In a shaker, mix apple juice, rum, vinegar, cinnamon stick and ice cubes.

2. Pour into a glass, then add kombucha.

Where to BUY this strange Stuff

BECAUSE NOT EVERYONE GETS TO RUB SHOULDERS with collectors of bacterial strains and kombucha mothers, we suggest a few virtual locations that will be happy to mail you the real stuff and everything you need to help it grow. These locations will also be happy to take your credit card number in exchange. But don't worry, we assure you that fermentation is not an expensive pastime: on the contrary, this expertise will enrich your life and save you money in the long run.

IN THE UNITED STATES

Culturesforhealth.com An excellent and comprehensive resource for equipment and cultures, along with answers to many questions (in the rare cases where you don't find the answers in this book!).

Gemcultures.com One of the major resources for everything to do with cultures.

IN CANADA

Revolutionfermentation.com Yes, our very own website, as of 2018! Here you'll find the recommended tools and cultures mentioned in this book and more.

Crudessence.com A useful resource for specialized tools and ferments, as well as all kinds of delicious products, fermented or not.

Mycoboutique.com Designed most of all for mushroom lovers, this well-established boutique also offers a good selection of equipment and ferments.

Mortierpilon.com To ferment in style, beautiful jars designed for home fermentations.

IN EUROPE

Brouwland.com A major European supplier of ferments and equipment of all kinds. Based in Belgium.

Also visit the **Fermentation Revolution** Facebook group to share recipes, successes, defeats, questions, photos, ideas — in short, anything fermented!

TIME for Gratitude

TO BE HONEST, THIS BOOK IS NOT ENTIRELY REPRESENTATIVE OF WHO WE ARE. It is far too attractive, well-crafted and orderly! If you're able to read it now, it's thanks to some truly amazing people who worked on it as if it were their very own.

For many reasons, especially for succeeding in giving the illusion that we have a fine, distinguished literary voice, for demonstrating patience and generosity in the face of our stupefying procrastination, for clarifying our ideas — which of course were ingenious, if somewhat scattered — the Golden Palm goes to Elizabeth, with our deepest gratitude. Without her, this book would have been a bunch of scribblings in a mason jar!

For having confidence in our passion, thanks to the gang at Les Éditions de l'Homme.

Thanks to Luce, for her presence, her honed artistic sense, her reassuring professionalism and, of course, her millions of colorful jars and napkins.

Thanks to Mathieu, for his talent in transforming a stain into visual poetry.

Thanks to Ann-Sophie, for her finesse and her ability to turn our creative chaos into a polished visual work that gives us shivers of delight.

Thanks to Scotty, for his forest root beer recipe that didn't make it into these pages but served as an inspiration to us.

Thanks to Max, for always being there, ready to help with anything to do with food, and for being funny.

Thanks to Sarah Maude, for encouraging our madness and putting up with our mess.

Thanks to Julie, for enduring an intense photo session in her home, for inventing two sweet recipes for this book and for having a smile each morning, even when yesterday's recipe continues to languish on the kitchen counter.

Thanks to Susan, who taught us that one can eat a pickle without having to explain why.

Thanks to Louis, because he has always encouraged our curiosity.

Thanks to all the people who showed up for the meetings we missed because of the book.

Index

Library and Archives Canada Cataloguing in Publication

Côté, David, 1982-
[Révolution fermentation. English]
   Fermentation revolution : 70 easy, healthy recipes for sauerkraut, kombucha, kimchi and more / Sébastien Bureau and David Côté.

Includes index.
Translation of: Révolution fermentation. ISBN 978-0-7788-0593-9 (softcover)

   1. Fermented foods. 2. Cooking (Fermented foods). 3. Cookbooks.
I. Bureau, Sébastien, 1985-, author II. Title. III. Title: Révolution fermentation. English.

TP371.44.C6713 2018   664'.024   C2018-900882-2